WHAT'S WRONG WITH U.S.?

By: Randy J. Machado

What's wrong with U.S.?

ACKNOWLEDGEMENTS

I would like to take this opportunity to thank the countless persons who have assisted me in this project; a work that started as a mere collection of random thoughts and has evolved into a focused piece of observations. Specifically, I would like to thank Looking Upwards, Inc., the James L. Maher Center, AVATAR, INC., Ocean State Community Resources and Bristol Community College for allowing me artistic license when developing and conducting trainings and lectures.

Further, I would like to thank the following for their assistance with editing and technical design; Patrick Boxx, Gloria Davis and Andre Faria.

Most importantly, I would like to thank all of the persons that I have supported in this field, as you have taught me a great deal more than I could ever think to teach you.

Table Of Contents

AN INTRODUCTION..........

Wh32at's wrong with you---huh? In fact, what's wrong with us? We are the almighty---the invincible superpower in the world, the moral and ethical experts---yet we find ourselves often questioning our motives, actions and behavior. We wonder why as resources, power and material collections increase, we seem to have more complications and difficulties. We are all lead to believe that if we acquire MORE and MORE, and elevate ourselves to a place of supreme confidence and autonomy, that things will get easier and life will be better—right? Wrong. Affluence and wealth does not equate to moral and ethical superiority. Nor does it imply a higher evolution of societal skills. It is often noted that the United States is one of the wealthiest nations in the world--- with some of the most severe and significant individual and societal issues. Why is that?

We need to examine what makes us psychologically tick in order to understand why MORE doesn't necessarily mean better, and why inflation of the self and collection of materials and power can lead to destructive behavior--- individually and collectively.

I want to tackle some of these very concerns by offering a profound and prolific analysis of the American way of life. I wish to analyze the behaviors, patterns and errors I have noted throughout the years---in us, as a general American society. I want to point out the obvious and the subconscious reasons to help explain "what has gone wrong with us."

My understanding of how circumstances go wrong for people on an INDIVIDUAL basis; when people find themselves in predicaments where they wonder, "why is this happening to me?," "what is going on in my life?," "what have I done wrong?," and on a SOCIETAL basis; when the lot of us ask ourselves, "what have we done?," "where have we gone wrong as a society?'" WHAT ARE

WE DOING TO OUR CHILDREN?" It is a very difficult thing for people to understand why things aren't going the way they should----particularly when one has followed all of the rules of engagement.

What are the rules of engagement you ask? The very rules and protocols that have been ingrained into our thought patterns about what makes one a successful American individual. The acquiring of wealth, status, power, esteem and superiority come to mind. Television, media, role models and even self help authors,' all discuss the importance of inflating the self to a position of confidence and autonomy. But none discuss how to behave once we arrive.

Self help guru's are abound to offer us assistance in acquiring wealth, independence and autonomy. In fact, it is written into the very constitution of this great country---"that every individual is born with certain inalienable rights and freedoms." What happens when the sense of the self becomes too strong, too powerful, and too superior? Last time I checked there exist no system where one's sense of the self can be measured. Nor is there any recommended system of correction if such an inflation were to be noted. When does it become too much and how are we to deal with ourselves when we get "too big for our britches?"

We often tell others who suffer from a low sense of themselves to "brighten up young man---think positively and confidently about yourself." So we begin as a matter of recommendation to correct these faults in our personalities, to embark on journeys of self exploration and esteem building. Once we begin to accumulate such credentials and gains, when are we to turn it off, stop and self examine to note whether we have grown enough to live humbly and confidently. To me, there seems no barometer to measure such gains and occurrences. This is a major problem in my opinion.

There are examples abound to note the errors in our maturation of the self in the United States; Hurricane Katrina, our involvement in Iraq, the Los Angeles riots, and the current behavior of our children to name a few. We all seem to "get" that there is something really wrong, but nobody can seem to put their finger on it. I hope to place my finger upon that very nerve, pluck it, agitate it and expose it for discussion and analysis.

My intention therefore; to offer a theoretical consideration of our human behavior; and to relate our behaviors to the more general and societal patterns that tend to grow and metastasize into larger and more complicated trends and movements. Societal patterns and trends unfortunately, that I believe are erroneous in nature and threaten our very way of life in the United States. Such movements that have been created by "us" and what we think of ourselves. Such similarities include patterns of individualism, egocentricism (self-centeredness), and patterns of societal and technological progression. All of which may lead to our own "self" destruction.

For example, I believe that we have developed a very particular and unique version of the self here in the United States. A self that is very egocentric---perhaps even bordering on the narcissistic. It is truly "all about us!"------at least that is what we believe. This is not true in others cultures around the world and I plan to explain the differences.

Further, changes in society and technology have had a dramatic and altering effect on the development of who we are and the children that we are raising. One only needs to look next door to see the qualitative differences in the way our children are behaving-----and the way we in turn treat our children. I plan to discuss these issues more specifically and individually because each merits significant discussion and review. More on this later.

....

The main "fuel" if you will that allows me to make such assertions about how we operate comes from my experiences and background in the field of Psychology.

It makes me laugh when people ask me why I do the work that I do, and what do I really get from it? I receive all extremes of appraisal of the work that I do. Some people say "you're a Godsend" and thank me---"you have been sent from heaven" they exclaim, "I don't think I could do it," "God bless you,"-----to, how challenging and rewarding this must be for you.

My response is always consistent; I like to tell people that my job is the most fantastic job in the world. I get to meet people from all different cultures and behavioral and "interactional" backgrounds, and get to see behavior in its truest form. Little do people know that I am always paying attention to how *they* behave.

My job involves providing behavioral and psychological supports to numerous Agencies in the Rhode Island area that support folks with developmental disabilities. Additionally, I am also an Adjunct Faculty Member of Psychology at a local community college in Massachusetts. As such, I am responsible and compensated to "pay attention" to behavior. To discover why people do what they do and what is "gotten/benefited" from such actions. Once learned, I am responsible to train others regarding these observations and tendencies so that they may recognize these actions and learn about themselves, negative behavior and psychology as a discipline.

I must say that I particularly enjoy teaching students and staff about themselves and what their human tendencies and inclinations are about. They, unfortunately, are not always pleased and excited to hear what I believe to be the truth about "us." Needless to say, it is what it is.

This, I believe is the lot and mission that I have been assigned in my life. Such tasks often come with a heavy dose of responsibility and necessary care. People are often looking to me for advice and guidance regarding behavior and how to interact with others. Therefore my responses need regular censure and monitoring to ensure that what I am observing and concluding is accurate and steadfast. I take this responsibility very seriously.

Said is not an easy task; however, what one begins to discover after a while are certain patterns of actions that we all have in common with one another. Such patterns can be healthy patterns or they may be destructive behaviors. Acts of kindness; transformations of groups from negative perspectives and actions to positive styles of interacting, would be examples of healthy patterns of behavior. Whereas the mistreatment of others on any level (and subsequent acceptance of this mistreatment), would be an example of negative behavioral patterns.

Regardless, behavioral ways of being are there for the taking----and, there for the observing and identifying. One only need to attend to these occurrences to note their existence. What is interesting to me is that these behavioral patterns will begin to reoccur over and over. Once practiced and preached these behavioral patterns or "ways of existing" can often become the status quo and preferred way of interacting---simply because it has been practiced and learned.

I know that sounds a bit odd, but when one examines how trends and movements begin to materialize, one can often point to a source or initial catalyst that began the process. Such occurs all the time. The civil rights movement and ending the suffrage of woman in this country would prove two good examples of this learned pattern of behavior. Treatment of people with color and women were quite different before these movements began. That is to say, this way of behaving was an accepted and expected way of interacting with others. Clearly a negative pattern of existence that was erroneous, and we as an American culture should be ashamed.

Once identified persons began to see it differently-----and began to behave in different ways, a trend and pattern began to emerge. Once this trend and pattern was practiced and encouraged, it began to take the form of "a way of being." Once a way of being, it became an accepted and expected way of being, therefore solidifying its existence for others to now practice in turn. Often this is a powerful and necessary transformation led by the few who recognize the need for change, and those who will eventually follow.

Speaking of which, it amazes me how many people will blindingly accept a practice or behavior just because said practice is the "expected practice or behavior." I believe this occurs because many are consumed with their own agendas and self needs and do not consider the significance of the practice. Only if the movement in some way impedes or conflicts with the needs of the self, does one attend to the specifics of the movement or practice. This is particularly true here in the United States. We attend to the things that the "self" believes to be important. Practicing trends, movements or ways of being are not always called into question by the self. It is only when one is raised with principled ethics and morality does such good intended needs become self needs, and therefore important to the self. Such examples may include the various movements that were discussed earlier.

In the case of the aforementioned example (following good practices), this is obviously a good thing— providing that the followers will follow the practice of good. Unfortunately, the reverse is also true; when those with ill intent endorse a movement that is negative, the same followers can often be found. The same could occur if the leaders of the movement are ignorant to the possible outcomes of a cause. In such cases bad things can occur, and others will blindingly follow without understanding.

Adolf Hitler and his manipulation of others would prove a great example of this process in action. People found themselves cheering and supporting a movement that later became the most horrific effort at genetic cleansing in all of history. As we would later learn, most of the Officer's in Hitler's regime later claimed that they were "just following orders' when instructed to slay mass numbers of innocent people. A set of practiced behaviors, which became learned behaviors, which became the status quo----which became an accepted way of existing. Scary heh? The people of Germany at the time were a crushed and defeated people so therefore concepts like the self and egocentricism were not important. Unity and the success of the whole were the main focus and Hitler was aware of this.

Stanley Milgram would later present to the world that we as human beings do in fact "just follow orders" when presented with the command to do so. If you recall, he designed an experiment where he attempted to confirm this notion of "just following orders." In brief, he manipulated college students and instructed them to shock an elderly man in another room with successive voltages of electricity each time the elderly gentleman answered a question incorrectly. Of course there were no real electric currents delivered, however the students were not aware of this. The results suggested-----rather overwhelmingly, that we as human beings will in fact follow the orders of a perceived authority figure when instructed to do so. Be afraid, be very afraid.

It's only when one questions such practices does a change in direction begin to occur. But how often does that really happen? Surely, the likes of Martin Luther King would be exempt from this statement.

Unfortunately, we have numerous examples of negative patterns of behavior that exist in today's world, particularly here in the United States. How we treat one another has become increasingly negative and judgmental, and much of our cognitive energy seems devoted to the self and indulgent thereof. This concentrated focus on the self is quickly becoming a "way of existence" that is accepted and taught to our children.

We see a growing class distinction between the wealthy/privileged and the poor and indigent, and we don't seem to be disturbed by this. I believe what is beginning to occur is a negative transformation to a demoralizing society. I also believe that this process has been festering for some time, slowly growing and materializing. Philosophers and theorists often identify that the end of all great societies is when morality and ethics disintegrate.

It is beginning to rear its ugly head and I believe that we should take note. I think we have been following along----much like cattle or sheep and have accepted these ways as "reality." It's time for one of these sheep to stray from the pack and make a statement----can I get a BAAAA please! Thank you.

The common denominators of such negative patterns seem twofold in my opinion; (1) the particular version of the self that has developed here in the United States (and the subconscious manifestation of this practice) and (2) the interplay between the self and our genetic pre-dispositions/commonality with our primitive behaviors. Peaked your interest---haven't I? The later will make more sense when I discuss "primitivism," and explain how our behavior during times of crises can make sense when considering the actions of others within a model of primitive behavior. That is, how can one who is ordinarily submissive, compliant and orderly, become aggressive, violent and extremely narcissistic? When the rug is pulled out from under him. When order and structure are gone and chaos ensues----and one is left with himself and the need to survive.

BUT FIRST.....................

In order for you to understand all of this, we need to first talk about behavior. What is behavior? Individually first and as a group secondly. When you really think about it, everything that we do, say, gesture, attempt in any sort of relationship---- with anyone or anything, involves behavior----everything is behavior. Connotatively defined, behavior is "any physical action or pattern of movement" however, any interaction or encounter that we have with anyone is going to involve some sort of behavior and response.

Simply stated, it is cause, effect and action. So I walk into the store and I see somebody that I haven't seen in awhile and say, "Hey Doug, how are you?" and he says, "Fine, how are you?"---I respond back based on what he has responded to me. It is very Skinnerian in that regard, in that we are all cause and effect for one another. If we remember, B.F. Skinner provided the world with an explanation of human behavior that suggested that we are all cause and effect for one another. He argued that overt patterns of behavior that are measurable and observable, should be the most important and relevant topics for Psychological study. One's emotions and inner thoughts were not as important in his world.

However, it can be more than that as well. It is paying attention to gestures, facial expressions, and other physical movements that may accompany the words. When I say hi to Doug, what's he look like when he is saying hi back to me? Why, because I get a read on that, I make internal conclusions based on his gestural responses. Therapists often say that "everything is communicated with your body." Whether you like it or not, you give it away. Said gestures and expressions are the overt/physical ways of describing and presenting our internal attitudes and opinions for the world to see.

Further, what types of behaviors and actions are expected at that particular time? I would argue that the responding behavior would be a product of one's particular culture and learned responses and attitudes of that particular culture. I am going to give the response that I am expected to give. When we begin to accumulate such responses and behaviors, we form opinions, attitudes and ways of existences. And sometimes, those ways of existence need to be called into question.

Further, such responses are often reinforced based on what is expected from one in a particular culture. Ordinarily, when one studies negative behavior and behavior challenges, one looks for the reinforcing agent that keeps the behavior alive and reoccurring. Often for little children for example, *escape* is a popular function of behavior.

The other day I was in the grocery store and saw a young mother struggling with her child because he was demanding candy from the cash register aisle. She of course stated "NO," and he of course began to protest. The altercation quickly grew ugly and the small child "kicked it up a notch." He looked around, arched his back slightly and with one felled swoop, threw himself onto the floor.

The child in this case was attempting to avoid (or escape) the demand of his mother. His first method of choice was to protest and cry. When that didn't work he chose to bring others into his plight for righteousness by making a huge spectacle out of himself-----and at the same time putting Mom on the spot. As the judging grandmothers looked anxiously on, Mom had to make a decision----"how do I deal with this?" Unfortunately for her she made the wrong choice, but the easiest way out. She gave in and allowed him to have the candy. All the judging grandmothers looked on in disappointment. Regardless, we all present with various behaviors throughout the course of a day, and most of those behaviors are met with some consequence; the behaviors that are punished tend not to survive, the ones that are reinforced, tend to live another day.

When repeated reinforcement for behavior is provided, it lives further and grows into a way, movement or tendency if you like. When such tendencies grow they become ways of living and existing. Such was the case with Hitler, such was the case with Martin Luther King and such is the way of today. The question becomes what will tomorrow bring? If that little boy continues to receive inappropriate reinforcement for his negative behavior, is allowed to *escape* repeatedly, said little boy will grow into a "big boy" who does doesn't like to hear the word "no." His level of protests will become a way of regularly behaving and existing.

So everything is behavior, and my responses to what is presented to me are going to be dictated by the prevailing "ways of existence" at the time. This, we should accept as a common phenomena in human existence. We have plentiful history and example of this process in action.

....

      Now that we got that out of the way, let's talk more specifically about how to "get" other people, to understand their behaviors and to understand what has gone wrong in our American culture. For this conversation it will be extremely helpful for us to become familiar with the concepts of individualism and egocentricism, and how that relates to the self----first and foremost. Egocentricism for our intents is defined as "self-centered" like behavior, with a primary concern for the self first and the group secondly.

      This initial definition of egocentricism and the self should not be viewed as a negative, as it serves an initial life function for survival and existence. In fact I believe that we are all born with this primary function toward the self to satisfy our basic physical needs. When I talk of the "Americanized version" of egocentricism and the self, it is there that I make the negative distinction between the two.

Individualism is defined as an inherited form of entitlement that has been generationally passed from our founding fathers. This I believe has triggered the focus onto the self and has elevated our "innate egocentricism" to its current state of the superior "Americanized version of the self" that is alive and well here in the United States.

So, in order for me to understand how another person is behaving or acting-----or why they are doing what they are doing, I must understand initially that the person is coming from a place of egocentrism (self centeredness) much the same way as I am. And, my fellow American---- much like myself, is a victim and recipient of the same level of entitlement (individualism) as I. Because we have been raised in this great country, with its great history of independence and autonomy, we have all been conditioned to understand that we are entitled to such independences and luxuries. This emphasis and teaching has produced this complicated creature which I call the "Americanized self."

If I can understand that-----I will understand their actions more clearly. This is a real fundamental principle that we must all "get."

Further, one needs to understand that these variables (individualism and egocentricism) are ways of being that are not always immediately apparent to the self. I believe that many thoughts and beliefs exist in the "subconscious," a state that is unaware to the self. That is, when one takes for granted a particular way of existence and simply acts or follows a set of actions without thought. Such actions I believe occur without notice; that is once I have completed a behavior often and regularly, I now complete this action without regard to active consideration for what I am doing. I believe such behaviors to exist without conscious awareness.

I also believe much of our behaviors and "ways of being and acting" have been practiced and now exist in automation. That is, we don't necessarily think about what we are doing, we are simply following along with the actions of others. The primary reason for this automation is the need for conformity and order. Without conformity, we would stand out among our peers, and this is not always a very comfortable position. In fact, it can be quite isolating to exist on ones own. Leaders of popular, ground breaking movements and changes were not very popular people in the beginning of their causes. Needless to say, it is much easier and automated to follow along with the others. In fact, it doesn't require a lot of thinking and conscious effort and allows us more time to focus on ourselves and our selfish needs.

I often discuss this automation in trainings, and explain to participants that there exists different levels of consciousness; the conscious mind, that is your awake, concrete, "what I see everyday things". The unconscious, for example, dream states and all that occurs when you are asleep, enter REM and dream. We are all fairly clear on the first two, however, we often forget that there exists a third state; the sub-conscious.

Sometimes we are not aware why we are behaving the way that we are. For example, you find yourself in the middle of a behavior/act, etc. that you know has been self-destructive for you, yet you're not quite sure how you got there. Sometimes you say or do things, and then question why you acted that way. Sometimes you follow the actions of others (conform) and later ask yourself why you did such a thing. The only exceptions may be alcohol and drug induced states and actions.

People have involved themselves in some of the most atrocious acts, and only later to realize just how awful it really was. Rape, accessory to murder and violence come to mind. The rape trial in Massachusetts in the early 1980's (Big Dan's) proved a good example of this process. A woman is raped in a bar with 3-4 on-lookers jeering her and egging him on. All are charged with accessory to rape, and are accused of "non-intervening" to stop the crime. All were conforming to the behaviors that were expected of them within that particular environment. Because that type of behavior is an action that one might witness in a bar environment, they all acted on automatic pilot and were steered by their subconscious.

Judgment is another good example of this process; how often have you offered opinion on a topic and suddenly noted that everyone was staring at you, unusually. The foot in the mouth effect if you will. You walk into a family Christmas party, and as you walk in the door your grandmother says from her perch on the couch, "Jesus, what did you gain 50 lbs---you're big as a house." Everyone immediately turns to see and size you up.

Did she mean to do this, or was this a "slip of judgment?" I believe that thoughts and behaviors often exist unrecognizably, subconsciously, and we take them for granted because they happen over time and we become accustomed and adapt. We allow them to become automated.

As a means of humor and levity I often compare judgment to a basic filtering system; that is, theoretically, we are all born with a basic filter that develops over time into a strong editor between our thoughts and what ultimately comes out of our mouths in the form of words. Judgmental statements occasionally slip through this filtering system, resulting in this "foot in mouth effect."

I believe the older we become, the more deteriorated this filter becomes, hence rendering it incapable of editing and catching these statements. I often joke and suggest that there are two times in life when we "tell it like it is;" once when we are toddlers because we don't know any better and our filters are still developing, and secondly when we are very old, because we just don't care anymore and our filters have disintegrated. Egocentricism and/or "a way one behaves" can occur within this subconscious realm. We often find ourselves operating according to our own "agendas" and motives, often unaware that we are even doing this.

....

Throughout the remainder of this text I will be discussing other variables and elements that I think make up who we are. I will also be discussing environmental issues and how one can adapt and change for the good, bad or different. I will explore primitive behavior; our basic instinctual process and encoding that exists within all of us, and how that interplays and shapes who we have become.

I will help you understand your interactions with others and how that differs from the general behavior of other people living in other countries. Why is their behavior different? What are the issues that are going on around them that may be affecting their interactions with one another? I will discuss all these paradoxical questions in more detail.

Toward the end of this vast philosophical exploration I will offer some functional suggestions that we as a society may consider------*consider* being the operative word. That is, any theoretical suggestion or concept in written form may remain just that---another idea that bursts onto the scene, is debated in intellectual forums and then is sentenced to a "life of shelf."

In the following text 3 important "phenomena" or variables are further discussed. Such concepts include Individualism, Egocentricism and Primitivism. At the conclusion of this discussion you will have a better understand of how we work as a human being first----and as an American second. If you are able to comprehend how these 3 principles interact with each other, it will be easy for you to guide and influence your relationships with others. You will understand where others are coming from, and why they are acting the way they are. You, in a sense, will become a "common sense scientist," ready to change and influence the world---hopefully for the good.

IN THE BEGINNING.........
A DICUSSION OF INDIVIDUALISM

Ohne of the specific topics that will contribute to our understanding of what is wrong with us is the evolution of American civilization; that is, the roots of our independence as a nation, and how that term independence has evolved and influenced the way we live in this country. It is very important that we understand where our basic opinions of ourselves have come from. For example, I need only reference this concept of independence and how it has attributed to some of the very difficulties and conflicts that we find ourselves involved.

That is, we tend to be very individualistic in our thinking, and this often proves contrary and oppositional to the way others in the world tend to operate and function as societies. Granted, variety is often the spice of life, and we are quite proud of our societal differences, however, one needs to ask, how much is too much, and when does a "way of existence" begin to feed on itself---- hence causing irreparable damage? Is it possible to become too individualistic? I believe this question to be a difficult one to answer as we are so accustomed and trained in the practice of independence. So much so that I believe it has developed into an "ism." To which I call Individualism.

Such is not the case when we examine other Countries and cultures. If, for example you were to travel to Europe, you would find many smaller countries grouped together within very close proximities. Consequently, there tends to be more of a sociological approach to how people exist with one another because they are so close. Given these physical proximities and constraints, they are forced to think in more of a group dynamic; that is, less about the self and more about the effect on the group.

I was recently conducting training where a German exchange staff person was present. Immediately following, he approached me and asked me to help him create a diversity training to assist with bridging the gap between "American staff" and "European staff." He suggested that the European staff were having difficulty relating to the American staff.

He further stated that Americans tended to become very offended when he offered feedback about training and their working habits in general. I asked him to expound on this concept, and he stated that in Germany, it is common for one to offer direct feedback to another for the good of the greater. That is, he stated, "for the efficiency of the whole" one needs to know how he or she is impacting others. This serendipitous occurrence couldn't have come at a better time, as I was in the middle of writing about this very subject of this unique version of individualism that has developed in the United States.

In other countries, there is no room for one to stretch in an independent fashion, and/or become particularly entitled about anything. In this country, starting with our founding fathers----including the revolt against what we thought was an injustice in the United Kingdom, we have always contemplated and believed ourselves to be individuals first, and part of a group secondary.

In history we know it as the Revolutionary War; where we as a colonized group of people in a new, spacious and abundant land, believed that we had certain unalienable rights and freedoms, and should not be subject to royal rules and proclamations. As such, we revolted and began a massive assault for "freedoms sake".

Also as we know, this great battle ensued for a very long time, and took a great many lives in the process. Not only had we adopted "individualism" and freedom as a theory, but we gave a great deal in resources, finances and lives in the process. Therefore, one could argue, great contributions on many levels were put forth to support and defend this philosophy. Also as we know, whenever one puts forth a great deal of time, resources and energy into anything, it becomes a big deal, a great movement and a lasting issue. This understanding is the very foundation for our way of existence in the United States. It is also I argue, one of the great contributors to the "modern day mess" within which we currently find ourselves.

I need only reference the repeated abuses of the constitution for self gain and manipulation. Such examples include the "bastardization" of freedom of speech that folks in the entertainment business site to justify the proliferation of inappropriate material to children. Movies and video games are a great example of this manipulation. Games showing adults fighting, murdering, running people over, inappropriate sexual content, etc. are fairly common place in all game rooms, software and video game stations. Movies showing the same are also common. My son or daughter can walk into any Mall, find the right section of any store, and have immediate access to inappropriate material.

Through process evolution, rumination and societal and generational focus and teaching, this initial obsession with independence (inherited from our founding fathers) has turned into a very individualistic, egocentric and self-centered approach to the American self. Freud would undoubtedly agree with this assertion, and may further argue that this type of focus and concentration tends to grow and sustain on itself; meaning that something that started as a revolutionary movement about the individual and what we felt we deserved; e.g., to make our own rules and regulations, constitutions and amendments, has turned into an ingraining of the stature and importance of the self. Inflated to a level that is "out of proportion" to what I think the original intent was.

I don't believe that our founding fathers could have imagined where this sense of the individual/self could have gone. I believe their intent was to have a nation that could live without royal rule and oppression from "dictator like" regimes, not to have the right to "expose children to inappropriate material" because it is our constitutional right to do so. This in my mind is a manipulation and a bastardization of the process. This process is so ingrained however, that I don't think we fully comprehend the dilemma. As the sense of myself as an individual grows, so does my sense of entitlement----meaning I believe that I am owed more and more, because it is my right as an American.

Freud may have called this process an "id explosion" or an "id feed." If we recall, Freud described the Id as the pleasure seeker, the uncapped and unmonitored monger of gratification. I believe that we live in a very "Id" rich country, both as a result of internal mechanism (being born a human being) and as a result of this generational feeding of the individual in the United States. American civilization has become about immediate gratification, about self centeredness and egocentrism.

When someone jokingly says to you, "you know it's all about you isn't it?" Well it is kind of all about you--- isn't it? That is, many of your thoughts, actions, behaviors and relations with others are based on the self. I often throw out, arbitrarily of course, a percentage as high as 90-95 % focus towards oneself. A singer once sang about this phenomenon when she exclaimed "what have you done for me lately." In fact, I often joke in trainings that many of the students in the class are probably more consumed with thoughts of what their next actions are to be, than they are about what I am trying to teach them. For example, I'll say, "you're wondering when is this class going to end because I have to stop at the store, call Johnny and I have to work at 3 pm.........." This usually gets a chuckle from all because I am usually right in this contention. In fact, I challenge you to think of any situation in which you have not acted in a way that was NOT about the self. Difficult isn't it. The funny part is that we are often incapable of recognizing when it is happening (remember that subconscious thing I talked about?).

We get into arguments with others all of the time. How much time do you spend considering the other persons perspective on the issue? Probably not much. The angrier you become, the more internal your thoughts become, and you begin to become real specific with particular information that backs your claim to "why you are right, and they are wrong."

I believe that this very proposition has contributed, fueled and ignited many of our conflicts with others and is an ongoing contributor to our troubles in relating with other countries in the world. What started as a necessary movement toward independence has bloomed; consequently manifesting, culminating and has grown to a point where we now believe individualism is something we are owed, not something we deserve.

Proof of the existence of this phenomena are plentiful abound. A classic example is the coming together of people following the 911 attacks. It amazed me, driving on the highways and seeing the sudden unity----- descriptions/words displayed on highways and overpasses such as "united we stand," "we shall protect the United States and all who threaten it, etc." Essentially it was a forcing of unity, a coming together as a group with one common cause, which was, in this case, to fight terrorism.

One cannot argue that we had gone from a very individualistic/self-centered culture to a sudden (arguably prodded) position where we needed to become a group----- and we needed to become a group quickly. The reason; we needed to combat something that people were very fearful was going to happen again-----terror in our home land. It was a threat to the very way of existence---arguably, the only conditions in which we as an American society would allow ourselves to become close to one another in a common cause.

This "coming together" however will be short lived, providing there is no impending, eminent threat or catastrophic event that occurs that forces us together again. We already see evidence of these phenomena in action, as we have grown tired of our occupancy in Iraq and no longer believe it to be necessary. Why? We must return to our individual pursuits and re-focus on ourselves. Ironically, the candidates for the 2008 presidency were using this very subject as the main source of debate----where's the irony you ask? Well, the fact that each individual candidate has an individual/self-centered perspective on this issue, and is egocentrically utilizing the subject to jeer their fellow candidates and the sitting president. The goal; self gain and promotion of the self at the expense of others. Long after this book is written, read and reviewed, the same process will have repeated itself 10 times over.

Terrorist groups, ironically enough would also term our fascination with the self as inappropriate, hence their claims of evilness, "the evil empire" and "satanic like" in our purposes and positions. I believe they are correct with their identification of self-centeredness and individualism and perhaps even correct in their position that we have become too expectorant and entitled. What I disagree with however, is the terrorist correlation between demonology and egocentricism (self centered behavior).

The reason; well, call it the "haves and the have nots," or simply call it a "deprived id," or perhaps an "immature or developing id." You see, we're not that much different when you examine all the issues within this framework of the self, and development thereof. It is not uncommon for one to seek refuge in groups, cults, religions, etc., when one finds themselves in positions of social isolation, deprivation and "individually poor statuses." Why, just as we needed to ban together as a group to combat terrorism, others are presented with a need to unite to combat their own examples of deprivation.

The difference; our episodes of unity are rare, unusual and only based out of necessity. Others episodes of unity are regular, consistent and a constant way of life and being. Why? Because the deprivation is much more significant and of a different flavor. We live in the land of the plentiful; go to a different country and note the differences. The amount and variety of food, the availability of material items, safety, justice systems and favorable social policies, would be a few differences that you would note.

Our egos and our "sense of the self" have grown so gigantically that we don't' even see it. It is not very difficult therefore to understand terrorism----one need only consider a culinary analogy; mix 1 large bowl of material deprivation with 2 cups of "id/self immaturity," stir to apple sauce consistency. Then add 1 cup of a unifying religion and a pinch of primitive behavior/instincts. Bake and/or allow to stew and fester for many years; the result Terrorism sulfate.

It is somewhat Maslownian in that, others (terrorists groups, material deprived countries), have needed to focus on the material and safety aspects of life. Where is the next meal coming from, will my family be safe today, etc. This continued focus and concentration of such, forces a depriving environment, which in turn forces a need for unity with others, and occasionally, a judging and envious relationship with those that are more developed and have more resources and materials. No rocket science here.

We have plentiful examples of people living in similar regions as the extremist terrorists groups that do not adopt the same terrorist policies. Why? Our friends in Saudi Arabia may be able to shed some light on the subject. No deprivation here, in fact they seem to be very pleased on what life has had to offer them----ironically enough, some of the same luxuries that we take for granted here in the United States.

That all aside, it interested me very much to see us all pulling together, almost subconscious to ourselves. One would have to conclude upon witnessing such actions that social psychologists interested in human behavior, sociologist's, and behavioral psychologist's must have had a field day with watching what happened during that process; when a culture obsessed with the self is forced to exist in an alternate or almost a confounding and contradictory manner in order to achieve a goal.

Arguably, our grandparents and elders understood this concept of unity far better than we are able to contemplate in today's American society. Unity and the collective working together were staples for young America pre and post-war. Depriving events early in the United States such as the Great Depression, etc., again provide an argument for this focus on the whole versus the self; we all banded together in our state of deprivation and misfortune and found console and commiseration with others. We all stood in the bread lines together and appreciated the fact that there was a loaf left for me once I arrived at the front of the line.

This also explains why our immediate elders are so critical of "our" way of life. "You should save your money," "I'll just get bread for dinner---did you see how much that chicken cost?" Maybe it's just me, but the older generation of folks seem much more "group orientated," conservative and appreciative then the younger generation. I believe this a result of experience. My grandparents and their families needed to engage in group activities for many reasons; there was a shortage of material goods, resources, etc., there was active war and uncertainty, and there was no advanced technology in which to engage oneself, so one was forced in a sense to communicate and participate with others.

This resulted in group activities and involvement and a consequential impact on how people thought of others. Feelings toward others have changed over the years because of this shift from the group to the individual. Now, I judge, make decisions and form opinions of others based of what "I" think first versus how it may affect you or others. The learned behaviors of our children are developing within this model. The result takes the form of insincerity and a disregard for others. When deprivation weans, and success and financial stability return, so does the concentration on the self. The longer the rumination and basking in such stability, the more powerful, entitled and righteous the "Americanized self" becomes. Words like "humble" and "humility" becomes terms of the past----and a negative, consequential effect on our morality follows suit.

Understanding issues like "Americanized" egocentrism, a spawn if you will from the beginnings of individualism, is one of the keys to understanding other people and helps to define "what is wrong with us" in today's society.

INDIVIDUALISM + EGOCENTRICISM = ?

Now, let's get into the meat of the matter. We've already discussed the beginnings of individualism, now we need to discuss egocentrism; or what most people refer to as self-centeredness and/or a focus on the self. We can further break it down into basic terms, for example what drives our actions, who are we about----- particularly here in the United States, but generally speaking as human beings first. Let us examine egocentricism on a more fundamental, theoretical level. Freud argued that from birth we are all born with a focus on the self. Initially, this need fulfills basic functions that are important for survival. We are born selfish because we need substance to survive; we cry to be fed, we cry to be attended to and held. This need is innate and human, and we all go through it---no exceptions. Freud also suggested that because we all start our journeys in the world in this manner, we are much more accustomed to operating in the world as adults in the same expecting manner. That is, our egocentric needs have changed from basic needs (crying for food and attention) to more complex, social needs like crying for adult affirmation, demanding to "get our way," and obtaining as many material items as we can before we die. The one with the most toys wins----right?

We are trained in a sense to be selfish and to look out for A-#1, namely ourselves. This explains some of the behavior we see with children as they mature and age and begin to move into the adult world. "Spare the rod, spoil the child" say the older folk. That is, some argue we need to be cautious to ensure we "hip check" children as they grow so as to not create monsters.

Developmentally, a child is born into the world and develops survival based behaviors to ensure life. As that child begins to mature, he naturally believes the world to be his "oyster" and begins to test the waters to see if the world will continue to bend in his favor----so that he may get all of his needs met. The needs become more complex; moving to social and behavioral needs, and the obtainment of unnecessary material items. If the world caters and bends to his needs, the child matures into an adult that expects more of the same. The difference? The child becomes an adult—he's bigger, badder and more convincing of his needs and wants---distorted and selfish as they may be.

Perhaps you have heard of the saying "small child—small problem, large child—large problem?" I believe that Freud was offering and suggesting that innately, by process of internal mechanism and geneticism, we begin our lives egocentrically. Subsequent environmentalism; aka fostering and nurturing, and/or deprivation and trauma, serves to predict one's outcome and presentation to the world. Therefore, one would have to argue that we all begin our journeys in the world similarly---what, who and how we ultimately present, depends on the vast environmental variables that are available to us. Such examples include religion, economics, parental styles, trauma, demographics, technology, etc.

Freud also argued that we tend to seek two general needs in our lives that define our goal of self-centeredness; that is, the insatiable needs for happiness and the avoidance of unhappiness. Now when one considers this proposition it does initially make sense; that is, much of our actions, behaviors and interactions with others tend to center around these two needs. This was one of Freud's strongest and most notable contentions. When you think of the different elements or obstacles that can potentially interfere with our happiness, we can easily provide examples of behavioral acts that are performed to either avoid, conquer and /or eliminate those intrusions to fulfill these two needs. We carry out these actions to satisfy our need for egocentricism.

Examples of potential obstacles to the servicing of these insatiable needs of happiness and the avoidance thereof, include Mother Nature, the environment, social isolation and the limitations of our own bodies.

Examples of Mother Nature may include earthquakes, hurricanes, tornadoes and tsunami's (to name a few), and the fact that we don't necessarily have a lot of control over these occurrences. Given our egocentric maturity and developed sense of entitlement (aka Americanized Egocentricism) we believe that we are entitled to learn of the possible occurrences of these phenomenons, BEFORE THEY ARE ABOUT TO HAPPEN.

In fact, we became quite disturbed following the recent tsunami that devastated the Thailand region because we weren't able to predict its occurrence. Visions were captured on video of people lounging by the pool with cocktails. Suddenly, a great wave overcomes the resort and literally sweeps people from the poolside to the ocean. One could argue that it was quite biblical in nature; the great hand of God comes sweeping across a beachfront of gluttony and excess and takes them all away in less than a minute.

This lack of predictive ability and control over formidable phenomena can and has, caused great discomfort and unhappiness for many---and quite frankly, we don't like it. It damages the self. It would not surprise me to see organized efforts to research and develop sophisticated technology to predict such occurrences in the future. Why? Well we believe ourselves to be entitled to an explanation as to why this occurred and when will it happen again. It really gets in the way if you know what I mean. After all, we were right in the middle of enjoying all that we deserve (gluttonous access the alcohol and pleasure), and it was all taken away that quickly. Again, we do not like this.

Advances in technology have allowed us to make the great assertion that all such occurrences are merely misunderstandings in science, and once understood can be avoided and prevented. I often remind people that there was once a time in civilization when we believed that all that was good was from the Lord, and all that was evil was from the Devil.

A tsunami would not have been a question of what scientific and environmental factors caused this; rather it would have been understood as displeasure from God. I am not advocating for a return to religiosity, but I do believe that advances in technology have fueled our opinions of ourselves and have contributed to this inflated sense of the self that I speak of. If we can explain away unpleasant occurrences to faults in science, we protect the self from damage, and are able to relish that much more in ourselves without disruption.

Once this travesty occurred, we instantly became concerned with the impact that it had on us first, and as a region secondly. And we proved another example of "having" to ban together to tend to the disruption, much like the aftermath of 911. Theoretically, I think we become uncomfortable with the idea that we as individual selves need to come together in a clean up effort or to deal with the loss of individual lives. It is only for the consolation it offers to the self, that coming together in an effort makes sense and is tolerable. How dare somebody do that to us! The sooner we can correct this disaster, the sooner we can return to the more important focus on ourselves. Again, I believe this process to be under subconscious control; that is, we are not always aware that we are engaging in such psychological actions.

Granted the loss of any life is tragic and traumatic, however, we believe it to be especially so here in American culture. Research into the death rates, murder statistics, and loss of life information from other parts of the world would astound many upon review. Not to say that others in the world do not grieve the loss of life, but safe to say that they are FAR more accustomed and acquainted with death than we are in the United States. We treat the death of an American citizen as a national offense---why is that?

People die all over the world, every second of every minute of every day, yet when an American dies, it should be considered a national event that everyone should honor. To me it seems a matter of convenience and selective ignoring. We know that a lot people are dying in the world every second, but how many of us really act upon making a change in this statistic. How many people do you know that go out of their way to contribute money to end poverty, death and famine in other countries? Jesus, we can't even tend to a homeless mother with small children lying on the sidewalk right in our backyard. Isn't this disturbing?

Yet when a radical group figures out a way to hammer Americans on their own soil, we think the world is going to end. The reality of the matter is that these types of events have been occurring in other parts of the world throughout history. The difference is that we have never really had to deal with such regular occurrences.

I think it is very comfortable and "convenient" for us to think in this manner. Out of sight, out of mind if you will. There is a reason other countries in the world actively protest the United States on a regular basis. How many times have we seen video of anti-US protestors burning the American flag, burning look alike presidential manikins while protesting our foreign relations policies? Well, maybe they have reason to be angry with us. Maybe many innocent lives have just been taken when we inadvertently bombed the hell out of a town in search of a ruthless dictator with "nuclear weapons" on his person.

Viewing such disturbing video would only add to the unhappiness of the situation, so we choose instead to put a positive spin on the content. American media and our favorite television news shows take care of this for us. They may minimize the happening and/or discredit the groups by referring to them as "militia" groups or "insurgencies," thus stripping them of any validity and making their causes seem insignificant and only designed to cause us unhappiness.

The same holds true with issues such as social isolation; that is, when one finds themselves in a position where they are either incapable of relating to others, or find themselves in an outcast role. Such occurrences cause unhappiness and are in direct conflict with our basic needs and feelings of entitlement regarding the obtainment and coveting of happiness. Not uncommon then to find one with this particular issue joining groups, cults, and religions that are commonly unconditional in their acceptance of others.

Most groups would fit this description, and consequently offer solace and a feeling of belonging with others. It is a simple equation; unconditional acceptance=feelings of belonging=avoidance of isolation=happiness=A CONTENTED SELF. This formula can be applied to similar groups around the world; in the United States the primary motive for joining such groups would be social isolation and an un-relatedness to others, in other countries the main motive for joining such groups may be more related to general issues of material deprivation (as was the case in the United States during the Great Depression). This makes sense when one tries to understand such cults and radical groups in the United States. Examples abound; Reverend Jones and his "kool-aid" crew, David Koresh and his rebel group, and the multiple groups, cults and organizations that offer unconditional acceptance, with no stipulations. If we accept the fact that we need not for material items, it's easy to understand that we would not need to ban together to combat this need.

Again, other countries have this need and consequently, we see unity in those countries as a result. In then United States, the need for banning together (minus disaster), begins to take a social form. Our basic needs are met, abundantly so, so we begin to contemplate other needs of the self. Often those needs become social and interactional. Koresh and Jones had a large following because as the "American self" becomes more entitled and larger, it becomes more likely that others will be ostracized and segregated. Consequently, it will become more difficult to join a clan of others because such clans become more exclusive and narrow.

Why? Well, as we become larger than life in our own eyes, we become more selective of those that may fit into that same category. This field becomes narrower because the criteria for entry are specific and complex. If you are fortunate enough to find "your clan" you are one of the lucky ones. There are millions of people in this country who cannot seem to find their clans, and typically turn to organized religion, fraternities and the like groups to meet this innate need to relate to others in a social manner, and to avoid this potential source of unhappiness. The more extreme examples, such as Koresh and Jones, were probably made up of extreme personalities whom had experienced extreme deprivation and social isolation beyond your common, everyday examples. This may also help to explain some of the "extreme behavior" you see such groups carry out. Koresh; violence, fire, destruction and an end to the clan. Jones; self-destruction via suicide and the promise of a better existence elsewhere.

It's an easy formula to understand; extreme personalities attract persons who have experienced extreme deprivation or ostracizing from others. Such persons are attracted to one another with their experiences as the common denominator, and their unconditional acceptance of one another as the glue. The result is often irrational and extreme behavior to retaliate against the clans who had segregated them.

We are beginning to see more groups like this on the horizon, but as the "Americanized self" grows and becomes more entitled and stronger, the groups start younger and prove more dangerous. Also such groups are not limited to meeting halls and formal fraternities, as the internet has provided a powerful meeting place for such groups, all from the individual comforts of home.

I can now sit in front of my computer and converse with ostracized and segregated people from around the world. And because pictures and honesty are not necessarily important, I can elaborate and make myself whomever I choose to be---wonderful isn't it. I can now commiserate with the many of thousands of people around the world who feel my pain, and want the same revenge that I want. I can fester, plan and develop elaborate schemes to establish my goals, and get instant feedback from my cohorts. The result? Irrational behavior, destruction, death and disaster. Sound familiar?

Well it should, there is plentiful history to exemplify this point---one only need look on the internet to find chat rooms, groups and sects that offer acceptance to people who feel "unacceptable." In fact, many of the most recent travesties in school settings have involved kids who have fit this description of social isolation, have joined a group fitting this condition via the internet, and have enacted a plan that caused significant harm to others ("the ostracizers"). Our sense of ourselves has grown so significantly, that we believe that revenge is the only option, at any cost. Considerations of violence, the impact on others or the potential harm to innocent bystanders all become a secondary thought.

One of the major concerns with this new tendency is the age of many of the new clan members. As this sense of the "Americanized self" grows and becomes powerful, the maturation of said process also occurs at younger and younger ages. As our children become more articulate, intelligent and entitled, we as adults continue to hand over adult control to our children. The result as we know can be quite disastrous.

A mass murder plan of a 10 year old is not as manacle and deviant as a mass murder plan from an adult. The results unfortunately are the same. An adult who develops a plan for mass murder is arguably a psychologically disordered person who feels entitled and wronged in some way. A child who enacts a plan of mass murder may just be immature, entitled and heavily influenced by the sensationalized actions of others.

Through our lessons as the responsible adults and the responsible society, we have taught this child that this is the appropriate action required. We just don't understand this yet.

The last potential source of unhappiness is this issue of the self and potential limitations thereof; issues such as cancers, cardiac issues, general health obstacles and the deterioration of the physical self as the body ages. Again, the self finds this extremely disturbing and we often subconsciously develop methods to avoid such disturbances, as they produce unhappiness.

For example, we invest millions of dollars to research cures, vaccinations and answers to fix human ailment, and hence produce happiness and extend the longevity of the self. We create physical adaptive equipment so that we may conquer the inevitable; eyeglasses to fix deteriorating eye sight, telescopes to see beyond the human capability, braces, crutches and prosthetic limbs to correct an ambulatory issue.

We even go so far as to contemplate techniques to bring the body back, once technology has advanced to the point of regeneration and reversal of such disorders. There was a recent debate and controversy in the press about a famous baseball player (Ted Williams) who's reported last wish was to be frozen, and subsequently revived, once technology had advanced to a place where such a feat could be considered. He enjoyed himself so much, that he wants to come back once we figure out that whole "immortality thing."

So we're always on this mission, this drive, to bring happiness in our lives and avoid unhappiness in the pursuits of the self; overtly and physically, as described above, and covertly as well. For example, Freud described phenomenon's such as powerful deflection, where we make light of our misery and our unhappiness by deflecting it, or suggesting that it is just bad luck and will go away eventually----- it will get better we tell ourselves.

We substitute satisfying activities for ourselves and engage in something that diminishes the effect of the unhappiness, as a means of avoidance and redirection. Many people for example, engage in busy work and hobbies – they feel stressed out so they garden, sew, knit, play games, etc., because it allows them the opportunity of avoidance and the potential to return the self to a happy state again.

Perhaps a more powerful example of a covert operation is the use of intoxicating substances like drugs and alcohol. This allows us to render ourselves insensitive to the effects of unhappiness, and in the process brings us that much closer to a feeling of happiness---albeit short lived and temporary, and often with consequences (like a headache the next day).

In his work, Freud takes a hard look at human existence and behavior and tries to explain why it is that we do the things that we do, and why we keep doing them. I question further, why is this Americanized version of the self never satisfied? I find it profound that these insatiable needs for happiness and the avoidance of unhappiness feed this beast of egocentrism and self-centeredness and prove never ending; we never really seem to reach a point where we say, "okay, oh we're here and now we're good, now we can move on and be happy." It never quite ends that way.

We continue with this incomprehensible process only for momentary satisfaction. We can think of a lot of accommodating examples to demonstrate this point, "you know, if I could only have _____ then I would be really happy, then life would be good for me." "If I could only get that new car, that new BMW---you know, the one that just came out, then I can be really happy and life would be good for me." Is this really true?

Examine those situations and you will find that the person buys the new BMW----and as great as this initially is, will quickly adapt, become desensitized to the new product, and will soon add it to his collection of items that have been taken for granted. Another toy in his collection if you will. This is a very interesting phenomenon to me. "If I could only pay off this credit card, life would be good for me and my family". Well, again you take out an equity line or a second mortgage on your home and you pay it off, you get a payment that you are more comfortable with-----but does your lifestyle and discretionary spending now increase as a result? Probably.

Generally speaking, the larger the budget, the larger the momentary satisfaction and the more "stuff" it takes to feed this larger craving. I often discuss this version of entitlement in my classes, and will ask students if they can recall a recent episode where they may have heard of an example demonstrating such behavior.

For example, a rock star comes to a city to perform a concert. He specifically requests from the hotel the penthouse suite, where he would like 14 dozen red roses, the temperature set at 68 degrees, and lights dimmed upon his entry. Upon arriving, everything is exactly as ordered except that the lights are not dimmed to specification. Seeing this, he storms out of the hotel like a pre-Madonna, swearing to never return.

Students will shake their heads in disbelief and will often suggest comments like, "can you believe that," "unbelievable." But is it really that unbelievable? I often remind them that we are all just as entitled as he, the only difference being the amount and level of entitlement--- which directly correlates with the size of one's budget. No different I often add, then one of us storming into Wal-Mart and demanding our money back because the item we purchased broke in the car.

I also tell them that if suddenly one of them were to win the lottery (say 160 million), and we were to visit them one year later, we would see profound changes, particularly as it relates to how entitled one feels about themselves. We are accustomed to "dreaming" what it would be like to be very wealthy, but we are not well practiced at the art.

It really cracks me up when I watch a person on television giving an interview because he/she just won 200 million in a lottery. One question is always asked----"are you going to do anything different?" The answer----"no, I'm not going to change a thing, I'm keeping my job, etc............" My response, "yeah right." Let's visit this person one year later and I can guarantee there will be substantial changes in this person's life. Their sense of entitlement, their sense of who they are and their level of egocentrism will have grown exponentially.

Reflections of the past will be just that, reflections on how it use to be. I am also sure that the person will have legitimate reasons for the changes, as we all as human beings (particularly persons with highly developed egos) can rationalize any behavior, change or action when it comes to defending the self. What makes me happy today may not tomorrow, and so forth. Lord knows that we as highly developed, "happiness seekers" can explain away any and all of our behavior, providing it leads back to a state of wellness and pleasure. Conversely, an alternate, unhappy state is just not acceptable.

My point; momentary satisfaction or happiness is achieved and is gone, and this insatiable need to move onto the next thing re-occurs. It is a forever hungry beast---much like heroin, the more you have, the more you want. So what is one do with all of us this----how do we combat this process? Can we look at ourselves and say, "Okay I accept the fact that I am egocentric, and that all my accomplishments may feel great initially but may wean quickly?"

Can I set goals for myself, experience that initial joy and sense of accomplishment and make it last? Is this really possible? Perhaps, I contend, if we begin to understand that we operate this way, perhaps we can begin to learn ways to savor these accomplishments and goals and not fall prey to this habitual cycle. We are after all, incredibly adaptive creatures, capable of adjusting to almost any conditions in any environment.

Maybe we can learn ways to make these feelings last a little longer and relish in the accomplishment and achievement. Savoring the moment, understanding what is occurring and that it's part of our human tendency to go through this process of seeking, gaining and conquering – seeking, gaining, conquering, etc. I bring this to your attention as I believe it to be a foundational, if not historical explanation of the self.

I often use Disney World as a good example of this process in action. Often I will hear people say, "hey we're going to Disney World in October---yep, gonna take the kids to the happiest place on earth." I grin to myself, because I know that the above is a likely scenario and series of events that will unfold once in Disney World. The few times that I have been I recall many a family traversing through the park, bickering, yelling at their kids, looking for "Johnny and Susie" who took off, complaining about the 800 deep lines and 50 minute wait times for popular rides and attractions.

This friends, is the real Disney World. Once there, people quickly realize this, and begin to complain about such conditions, again because it is a source of unhappiness and an assault against the self and one's needs at the moment. Disney is fairly good at recognizing this cycle, and offers frequent doses of excitement between the unhappiness, to keep folks coming back in search for such doses.

Remedies to the long lines for example---"the fast pass," and the relentless happy, Disney tunes which we find ourselves humming all the way back to Rhode Island. The methodology; pack as many people into a park as possible, but attempt to maintain and satisfy everyone's insatiable need for 24 hour happiness and pleasure. This is no accident folks, nor is it a simple task to accomplish.

Combine the above with the inevitable and unavoidable interactions with others and we have a walking clash of egocentrism, each with their own agendas and missions, each believing their agenda more important, unique and special. This would help to explain the numerous difficulties people have with one another, often upon first impression. People get into arguments in stores, they fight over parking spaces, and they assume every action thwarted toward them is an act of aggression, rudeness or arrogance----is it? How dare that woman cut in front me at the "it's a small world" ride? Doesn't she know that this is the happiest place on earth, and that she is interrupting my individual search for happiness? We may not say these exact words when complaining about such an issue, but this is essentially what we mean.

The more egocentric and entitled we become, the more significant this problem becomes. "I can't believe that woman pushed her way into the aisle in front of me to grab the milk before I did---how rude!" Well, is this person a horrible, evil creature that's out to get her, or does this woman believe somehow, someway that she was intruded on in some way, shape or form.

I am sure if you interviewed both of those people separately they'll both tell a story on how the other person was invading their space and somehow violated their rights. We're just not able to recognize this phenomena---that we are all operating the same way, and that we are incapable of seeing it in one another. I don't know if that is irony or if it's an oxymoron-------- or if it's just plain humor.

We all seem to be functioning independently of one another, all thinking that our plans, ideas and missions are unique and special. What's even more comical is that we group others and their causes together, that they are part of _____ group that engage in this type of behavior. "Don't you hate those people who just push their way right through a line with no regard for anyone else?" I am the most special, unique person I know---according to me that is.

Advertising is particularly shrewd in this manner because corporations recognize this growing tendency toward the self, and reinforce and capitalize on its existence. They have Psychologists and marketing folks with psychological backgrounds working for them. Their job----- simple; devise methods, schemes and marketing plans with the above in mind.

If I can develop a plan that targets you as a special individual with particular circumstances and needs, then I can sell you a pretty red bridge that has a water view. Why do thousands of people converge on Disney world theme parks every day? Each has been led to believe that their family is special and is about to "discover the magic." When they arrive they discover just how special they really are---particularly when they meet up with the 60,000 other families who are "discovering the magic" with them (side by side if you will in a line).

Yes folks, unfortunately we are subject to regular doses of manipulation on a daily basis----all stemming from our growing selfish, egocentric presentation. Advertisement is effectively using our sense of self against us. "Are you tired of being left out---feel like others just don't understand you?" Introducing "e-dating," we'll match you with someone who understands you and is meant for you. Just send 8 easy payments of $49.95 to "e-dating.com" and we'll mail you your first list of personal matches. Money back guaranteed. And wait, if you act now, we'll also send you "the complete guide to the self" by Bernie Schister as a free gift.

What better way to capitalize on an egocentric society than to make egocentric people believe that they are individual, different and should be catered to in a special way. A sure fire way to make a boat load of money. All corporations are practicing this model, but nobody would want you to know about it. Gee---I wonder why?

Casino's cater to the self; free drinks, personal service, free buffets, etc all equal more time spent in the casino, equaling more revenue. How special do you feel when concierge service is offered, when tickets are purchased for you and reservations are made in advance? Now that's service isn't it?

Unfortunately however, it's all about the mighty dollar and not about you as a special person. I once conducted an informal experiment when I was in Las Vegas for a short stay. I walked over to the "dollar slot" machines and began playing. I suddenly had a craving for an alcoholic beverage and had heard that Casinos had typically offered its patrons free drinks as a courteousy. So, believing myself entitled to have a free alcoholic beverage, I began inquiring for such. Waitress after waitress after waitress walked by and ignored and/or shrugged off my repeated requests for a drink. I simply could not understand why.

Being the inquisitive young fellow that I am, I decided to walk over to the black jack tables ($25.00 minimum bet) and began playing. Well, much to my amazement I suddenly had a waitress on each shoulder asking me what I would like to drink. I had a choice if you will of which waitress I could choose to bring me my entitled alcoholic beverage---that I had coming. "That's more like it," I thought.

I learned a harsh reality that day----it really wasn't all about me as I had previously thought. It was about the almighty dollar. It doesn't surprise me therefore that those with abundant amounts of "moola" enjoy treatment that serves to expand this entitled sense of the self, and as a result become more entitled and "unique" in their own minds. Ever hear of the saying "sure Jim, you are a legend in your own mind."

Grocery stores are also guilty of this manipulation. Most stage their environments to make you feel comfortable—perhaps the store is a bit warmer in the afternoon, and is playing "golden oldies" on the music system because it knows that the senior's come in at that time of the day. Perhaps the temperature is lowered around dinner time and the music changes to top 40 because the store knows that the younger generation is getting off from work and will be stopping there on the way home.

Again, the more comfortable you feel in an environment, the more likely it is that you will stay. The longer you stay, the more you will spend. Brilliant. And my personal favorite; putting the milk and the bread in the furthest corner of the grocery store. You now have to walk by everything twice, to get the milk and the bread. Brilliant. Who can walk by all those groceries on the way there and back, and not buy anything they don't need? Not me. I would venture to bet that all of those "end slot positions" at the end of the isles on the way to the milk and bread are also for sale. My guess would be that you wouldn't find "store brand" tortilla chips here.

Commercials are particular good at this skill as well. Watch a typical commercial and tell me what you see. Is it reality or a necessary break from reality? A wise man (sorry I don't recall who said it) once said that Television was a necessary distraction from reality. That is after a long arduous day in the real world, we need a good dose of an altered reality to recharge are "egocentric batteries." Perhaps, I guess to remind us of how it should be for us----not how it is.

Essentially, when we watch TV we are watching an altered state of reality where everything is beautiful and typically works out for the folks involved. Just your typical everyday occurrence---right? For example, suddenly you see a commercial depicting 2 beautiful people, married (actors by the way), with 2 beautiful children (a boy and a girl of course), and all are home during the day (because they are independently wealthy of course). The commercial shows them strolling about in their 1.5 million dollar house---spacious and beautiful.

Suddenly they all decide to go (happily) for a run in the back acreage of their house---again because they are independently wealthy. Accidentally, one of the small, beautiful children falls and gets a nasty grass stain on his pants. No biggie----they all laugh and happily run back toward the house.

Suddenly the cameras pans toward the laundry room and shows Mom and the children "happily" throwing the damaged pants into the washer. Without warning, the camera shines on a glowing, illuminated box of laundry detergent. Now, everything will be OK, and the family can back to their "happy ways." This is commercialism folks.

Corporations know that if they can associate their products with perfect displays of happiness, wealth and beauty (what we all know we deserve) that we will flock to the markets like cattle to purchase said products. Why? Because we all want to be happy, forever so----without disruption. We want to be that happy family on TV where everything works out and nothing is out of place. We are always chasing this insatiable need for a happy self.

Subconsciously therefore, when we are walking through the grocery store and we come upon such a product, we suddenly feel compelled to purchase the item. Just like magic. This is another issue I believe that exists on the subconscious level, like judgment, where we may not necessarily be aware of the process but are succumbed to its effects. Some folks would call it subliminal.

The field of Psychology is full of interesting occurrences like this. For example, there exists an interesting phenomenon called the **fundamental attribution error**. I believe that this occurrence or tendency is used to defend the belief that we are special and unique, and our experiences cannot be described as common and "what other people do."

That is, we tend to attribute and describe any sort of negative action displayed by another person as a personality flaw----a negative characteristic about their basic person. However, if we are attempting to explain the same fault or the same error that we have made, we typically explain that error in terms of external events that caused its occurrence. After all, we believe ourselves impervious to such common occurrences and faults. Something outside of my control must have made this happened, "that Susie though, she is weak, etc."

This is a very well established phenomenon in Psychology; my question has always been however, is it an independent phenomena, or part of this description of egocentricism and the "American self" that I have described above? Let's say for example, you're having Thanksgiving dinner at your home and you're waiting for Aunt Sally to show up. Now, Aunt Sally is late and she was due to be there at noon. Here it is 12:45, and everybody is sitting around the table looking at the turkey, salivating, inching, grabbing their forks, wanting so badly to dig in but they can't because they have to wait----it's not polite to eat unless Aunt Sally has arrived.

The clock turns to 12:50 then suddenly someone makes the statement, "Aunt Sally is always late, she has always been late and always will be late, it's part of who she is. She'll be late for her own funeral." The statement therefore is that Aunt Sally is this late creature, this late being; it's just who she is-----a personality flaw, a negative characteristic that's personal and, quite frankly, not very nice. Now when Aunt Sally arrives, say at 1:00 p.m., an hour late, she walks in the door and says, "I'm sorry I'm late I got stuck in traffic, my alarm clock didn't go off, etc."

She doesn't say I'm a nasty, rotten creature and that's the reason for my tardiness. Based on her own egocentric need to protect the self, maintain happiness and avoid unhappiness, she explains away her tardiness and suggests an external cause for the occurrence (e.g., traffic). You see, when we're explaining challenging behavior of other people, we tend to explain it as negative attributes, something fundamentally wrong and rotten about the person. It's easy for us to do because we don't recognize our own self-centeredness and self needs at that time.

What is my need? My need at that time is to eat turkey; to gratify myself, to eat at that particular moment because I'm hungry. I don't see Aunt Sally as having gratifying needs of her own and so I attack Aunt Sally, and do so suggesting internal reasons for her behavior. That the actions were purposeful, intentional and manacle because they have affected me and my egocentric needs of the moment.

Aunt Sally on the other hand, innocently proclaims that it wasn't her fault; if she had, she would inflict damage to the self. One only needs to pay attention to everyday conversations and interactions to see this phenomenon in action---it is quite common. We tend to defend our egocentrism at any cost, usually at the expense of other people. I can guarantee you that the next conversation that you find yourself having will have the following conditions; (1) will probably reference someone who is not in the room (2) will involve a description about that person (either negative or positive) and (3) the descriptions will be internal descriptions describing personality characteristics to explain that persons behavior.

I can also predict that during the course of that conversation, you or the person with whom you are conversing will then compare yourself to said person, with you explaining away the same behavior and blaming external events that caused it to happen. We are such interesting creatures aren't we?

In fact, much of television today is an example of these phenomena in action; comedy for example, has become more about making fun of others, usually in a sarcastic manner. This method of communication has its roots in this fundamental error and in the emerging sense of the self that has been developing in this Country. The problem is that it is becoming more of a problem.

When we engage in this type of segregation and persecution of others at their expense, we add to their level of unhappiness---which they in turn seek to avoid, protecting their own individualized self. This was not the case in the times of our elders.

For example, early television and comedy in the 1900's was more about making fun of the self, or slapstick humor (e.g., I love Lucy, The Three Stooges, etc.). Moe would slap Curly and he would fall to the ground. Ricky Ricardo would poke fun at himself and everyone would laugh. We should all be afraid of this movement toward sarcasm, and the attacks on others as our main source of comedy.

Understand that this is what we are teaching our children. Nobody should be surprised when we see such actions like bullying and hazing increase in this country. Nor should we be shocked when we see drastic reactions taken by others when confronted with such actions like bullying and hazing; Columbine ring a bell? Classic demonstrations of the "American self" in action.

A child is ostracized because they are different (overweight, unattractive, etc.). This represents deprivation from others and a major source of unhappiness, so the child seeks to rid oneself of this unhappiness and deprivation by seeking refuge in groups of similar persons that will unconditionally accept them and make them stand out as a unique entity. Often these groups will appear very "brightly" and may have as a mission and theme, destruction and aggression (with its roots in anger from the initial ostracizing). They may dress in black, claim to destructive and aggressive and may be prone to violent and unpredictable acts. All is done to protect the self from unhappiness and deprivation.

Unfortunately, the above combined with youthful judgment and maturity often produces irrational behavior and the carrying out of such threats and actions. The result; Columbine----and the various replicas that have since followed. If you remember Columbine was the first major example of a child taking irrational matters into his own hands. Children walk into a school with assault rifles and unload on everyone and everything in sight. What we don't realize as a nation is that we have created this very phenomenon that we struggle to understand---and further reinforce this method of action and behavior by sensationalizing each occurrence with massive media attention and coverage, further glamorizing its use.

All things considered, this paints a fairly negative picture of the self and our motives. My intention is not to sound negative, but to sound real. I want to open eyes and present a view of human nature that makes sense and reflects what is really happening in our world today. Once we understand these concepts and processes it may help to correct some of the inter-relational problems we have with other people, and may force us to take a hard look at ourselves and what we are creating for our future.

Some people may argue with the above and suggest that we as a human species are not just egocentric and individualistic; there are such terms as altruism, selflessness and kindness-----for the sense of kindness.

Does altruism really exist? Do we engage in selfless acts with no expectation of return?

Proponents of this notion may cite entrepreneurs, wealthy people donating money, giving back to society. People completing heroic acts without thinking; endangering themselves to the point of potential death---all for the betterment of the person and with no regard for the self.

Now, I have to let you know that there are two camps on this particular subject. There are the humanistic folks that believe that altruism really does exist, that there is selflessness in this world and that people will complete kind acts with no expectation of gain. There's also a camp that believes that nothing is gotten for nothing, and that is there is no act that's completed without expectation of gain. I usually discuss this issue in training, and I ask people tell me someone or something that they believe to be selfless. On one occasion someone said Mother Theresa. "Mother Theresa is someone who demonstrates, exemplifies the concept of altruism because she has done so much with no expectation of any gain whatsoever"---this person exclaimed.

Now to some extent it's easy to buy that argument, it's easy to think "yes, that's true because Mother Theresa was a very giving woman." She did not care for material items, money, or self-promotion-----often to her own detriment and personal suffering. The altruistic camp would agree with this assertion and would argue that altruism does exist ------it's not always about egocentrism, gain and gratification, there does exist selflessness and selfless acts.

The behavioral camp however would argue that everybody gains something from everything------and that even Mother Theresa's actions can be considered within this egocentric model. What does Mother Theresa gain you ask? Some people would argue that Mother Theresa gains closeness to God, that's her motivation-----that's her gain. What is gotten from her actions is her expectation and belief that these actions will bring her closer to the Almighty himself. I tell you this not to cause controversy, disbelief in religion or dismay, but to inform you of both sides of the argument. To open your eyes to these issues of self-centeredness and egocentrism, and how powerful of a driving force it is in all of our lives.

I suppose if I had to take a position on the matter, I would have to agree that altruism/selflessness does exist, but is rare. Abraham Maslow talked quite extensively about altruism, or what he called self-actualization, and he also argued that the phenomenon is rare and only 1% of the population actually reach this level.

Maslow talked about a pyramid approach to life, arguing that where you are in your life right now, dictates how you present yourself to the world. For example, your income level, where you're living-----are your basic needs like food, shelter and safety met. If you are living in an existence that is deprived, unsafe, and dangerous, this will determine how you are going to be in the world, how you are going to approach the world, what your attitude will be----your happiness, sadness, etc.

He talked about the top of the pyramid as self actualization, where he believes 1% of the population of the world may inhabit. Selfless acts unfortunately are hard to find because we always feel the need to expose them, sensationalize them and in the process, make them "selfish" again. The mere fact that I am about to tell you this story right now, makes what I am about to say selfish, and no longer selfless.

As I have stated in the "about the author" section, I often find myself in workshops serving persons with developmentally disabilities. On occasion, I enjoy purchasing a soda from the soda machine. Soda unfortunately, is kind of like a drug in these workshops because many of the folks that attend are indigent and do not have a lot of access to preferred beverages like soda. So, being the giving, selfless person that I can occasionally be, I will often throw a dollar into the soda machine and will leave the 50 cents change in the drop container at the bottom of the machine for someone to find. Why? Well, I know that there are a number of people who regularly check this dispenser hoping that one time they will find 50 cents and can purchase a soda.

I think to myself, how exciting for this person to come along----having probably been denied multiple times, and he/she strikes the jackpot. Now, having never told anybody that story makes this act selfless and altruistic, with no expectation of gain and return. Having now written it makes it selfish and not selfless any longer.

Why? Well, having just read this passage, perhaps you thought, "well isn't he a nice guy for doing that," "isn't he thoughtful"-----in other words, you have provided me with a gain from my action and I have been reinforced for that behavior. Tricky I know, but true nevertheless.

PRIMITIVISM.......

Can the concepts of egocentricism and individualism describe and account for all of our behavior? Are there other variables that need consideration and discussion? I believe there are; one such variable or phenomenon is primitivism, to which I define as our genetic relations with our Neanderthal ancestry.

In order to understand how primitive behavior can have an effect on our behavior and our relationships with other people we first have to understand the basic dynamic of instinctual **inheritivism.** Meaning that we have all inherited a predisposition or encoding of Neanderthal behavior; mannerisms that lie just below the surface of our social behavior. The "genetic junk" if you will, that has been passed down from millions of years of Neanderthal existence.

When I conduct trainings for example, I often try to get everyone to focus on the prospect that we have much more genetic material floating in our bodies that is related to our Neanderthal ancestors than we do with our social ancestors. Social ancestors are fairly young in our existence----meaning our speaking ancestors, the politeness and all of the social graces that we enjoy on an everyday basis.

For example, I am speaking into a recorder right now driving in my car and enjoying the behavior of our social ancestors. I'm coming upon a light and it turns yellow to inform me that it is time for me to slow down and I, cordially stop and politely let the person who is waiting on the other side to go.

Similar happenings occur all the time. I will open the door for you when you walk into the store "please, after you", "thank you." All of these acts of politeness and social graces are relatively young in our existence. Conversely, I believe there exists in all of us a heavy genetic relatedness to our Neanderthal ancestors; we have much more documentation and evidence suggesting this proposition. Millions of years of genetic passing and encoding of these characteristics, in part, make up a portion of who we are.

Consequently what that means for us, is that much of those genetic vulnerabilities exists just below the surface. Primitive psychology would invariably agree with this proposition. It also seems sensible to me that if one has such a heavy genetic make up with such experiences, that it wouldn't be atypical to see this manifestation rear its head when the situation calls for such behavior.

When I give this example in trainings, it becomes humorous because people struggle with this assertion and say, "hmm, I don't know if I necessarily agree with that." Then I try to make the comparison and the analogy between common day events and a Neanderthal type of event. I know that sounds a bit ridiculous---but I ask people to examine the Katrina catastrophe and compare that event to a Neanderthal event.

Now in the absence of social order, and arguably there was no social order when Katrina hit New Orleans, I asked people to describe the behaviors they had known to occur in this environment---specifically in the dome, once we had corralled everyone to one location. Some of the answers that come from this question include rape, looting, violence and aggression. I say, "okay"-- those answers are fairly consistent with the hundreds of people I have trained. Then I ask them to tell me what they think the typical behaviors were around a campfire millions of years ago in "Neanderthals land;" that is, Neanderthal men and women sitting around a campfire on an average day.

What types of behaviors might you witness on any given 24 hour period? They chuckle at first then they say, "hmmm, stealing (okay that's looting), aggression, and rape". So I ask you, what's different?

I then make the comparison between Neanderthal behavior and common day behavior; the difference---- common day behavior is hidden within a blanket of social grace and order, a façade if you will. Deep within and readily available (unfortunately) are all these behaviors that I just described. The more depressed and intolerable the environment, the more likely you are to find primitive behavior. That is an interesting correlation to me because it helps me to understand a lot about our behavior.

Interestingly I was doing a training recently and I brought up this whole subject of primitive behavior and its effect on our common day behavior. One participant raised his hand and said, "I believe that we are just animals that have been around too long and have grown into something that wasn't intended to be". I thought that to be a fairly profound statement. Are we just sophisticated animals?

In order for us to understand how primitive instincts affect our behavior, particularly as it relates to primitivism, we need to discuss what I call the "survival cycle." I talk about the survival cycle a lot in my trainings to try to get people to understand that individuals are going to respond based on the environments in which they find themselves in.

So, if you can pictorially and mentally envision in your head as you are reading this, a circular diagram with the top of the diagram being the word environment; I often put the word deprivation in front of the this word because it clarifies the circumstances where one would need to enact certain behaviors in order to survive. At the top we have the words depriving environment; to the immediate right an arrow to the word necessity or necessary action. Following, an arrow pointing to behavior or behavior and action. Then an arrow to survival and another arrow leading back to depriving environment, hence completing the circle. That completes what I call a survival cycle; when one finds themselves in an environment that is depriving, one is going to engage in necessary behavior and action in order to survive.

I often reference the movie "Alive" in my trainings. If you don't remember the movie "Alive," it portrayed a rugby team that goes down in the Andes mountain range. The nice thing about the Andes is that it is very, very cold---- and the bad thing about the Andes is that it is very, very cold---"refrigerant like" one might say. Regardless, this particular group of people found themselves in the position where they were running out of food and they needed to consider whether or not they would eat human flesh to survive.

Now I posed this question to my participants in trainings and ask them the following question, "If you absolutely had to, would you or could you eat human flesh?" As an interesting aside, I asked that question once in training and one participant said, "You mean again?" I said that's too much information and I don't need to know that.

Joking aside, I usually get maybe one or two people that will raise their hand and say," yes, I would eat human flesh if I had to---to survive." I often point out to the rest that don't raise their hands (because most don't), that such a question is a difficult one to contemplate given their current circumstances; that is, everybody sitting around with coffee cups, bagels and muffins in front of them, fresh off of breakfast.

One cannot possibly consider what one's behavior and responses would be based on a full stomach. Go two weeks without food and I think one's attitude and behavior may change, some would argue radically. This phenomenon I call the survival cycle plays a critical and powerful role in all of our existence, and is often overlooked and taken for granted. It only comes to light when we are faced with a depriving circumstance. I personally think that we are not fully aware how powerful primitive instincts are and what an important role they play in our everyday behavior.

We have example after example of how quick primitive instincts can surface, and how they can affect situational outcomes and behavior. As mentioned Katrina and the Los Angles riots to name a couple. We can't also forget that we as human beings are incredibly adaptive creatures; we can adapt to almost any circumstance and any environment very, very quickly. We further present with the capability to rationalize all of our behavior once acclimated to such environments, usually in fulfillment of our egocentric and self needs.

I work with many people who have spent forty, fifty, sixty years in institutional living----a representation of having to adapt one's behavior in order to survive in a depriving environment. Such environments were Darwinian types of environments; that is a survival of the fittest, a dog eats dog type kind of world, much like the prison systems of today.

I argue that many of the challenging behaviors that I witness today from such folks, are often rooted, developed and born within the confines of such environmental experiences and conditions. If one is forced to engage in such behaviors long enough, hence representing "a practicing of such behaviors," then those behaviors become learned behaviors and can be very difficult to satiate or to modify. Behaviors such as aggression, delay of gratification issues and self-centeredness can also be a result of living in such depriving and abusive environments. Much like we discussed in the beginning of this text, that once certain behaviors are practiced and reinforced, they become a way of existing in an environment.

Imagine if suddenly you were picked up by your shirt collar and dropped in the middle of a maximum security prison in the middle of nowhere. One year later, we return and retrieve you-------I can guarantee that you're behavior would have changed. Why, because you would have found yourself in the middle of this survival cycle, dropped into an environment that was depriving, violent and primitive.

You would have quickly adapted your behavior to meet your innate needs for survival and preservation of the self. Your value system, moral and ethical codes of conduct and like social graces would quickly dissipate, and you would become instantly obsessed with yourself and your survival.

Interestingly, fifty, sixty years ago prison systems were about survival of the fittest per individual---- now it's become about survival of the fittest per the more powerful gang or gang members. It remains Darwinian nonetheless, in that we need to complete and engage in certain behaviors to survive the environments we find ourselves.

COMBINE THE THREE AND WHAT DO
YOU SEE........

My family and I will often find ourselves out to dinner. Usually, I will find someone or something that I need to figure out, analyze and describe to my family why such is occurring. As you would imagine, this can become quite cumbersome and intolerable. My wife will often say, "Can't you ever just turn it off and stop." "No wonder you can't sleep at night---

you never turn your brain off." But unfortunately, I just can't stop----I think I need a 12 step program for the "overnalyzers." I hope I have infected you with such a burden---that is, perhaps now we will all begin to analyze others and understand what is occurring. I challenge you to find this interplay of occurrences and begin a movement of behavior change for the better.

Anyway, on one occasion we are out having dinner and there's this guy at the next table with his family and their ordering dinner. Now, just as the food arrives— what I call the climax of going out to dinner, a peculiar behavior occurs. Arguably, when your food arrives at the table your mind is devoid of all thoughts and intentions, because you are focused on the very primitive task of eating and replenishment. You are not focused therefore on any conscious movement or behavior at this time.

Well, just as he is ready to dig into his food, he slowly, subconsciously, wraps his arm around his food in a protective manner, as if to guard against potential enemies. So of course, I point this out to my family and state, "ah ha---see I told you there was something about him----that man has been incarcerated or institutionalized at some point in his life.

He has learned behavior to survive in an environment, and now that behavior has become part of his very being, almost subconscious to himself." He isn't even aware that he is acting that way---"isn't that interesting?" My family typically responds by stating, "Stop that, don't you ever stop---you're embarrassing me." But you know what? I'm right.

We wonder why children who grow up in massively abusive environments act the way that they act. People truly do not realize what they are doing to their children by exposing them to certain conditions and environments. We are providing the templates for behavior, attitudes, opinions and ways of being for generations to come. I really don't think we know how important we really are in the eventual maturation of a child. Perhaps we're too focused on ourselves to see it.

Cycles are perpetuated; children grow to imitate what they have learned, primarily because this is all they know. The man who wrapped his arm around his food does this action because he has probably had to do this for a very long period of time---if he didn't, he didn't eat. Plain and simple as that. If he had to do this behavior long enough, this behavior and action become ingrained, subconscious and is now done without his direct awareness.

We should pay attention to this occurrence because it can explain much of the behaviors, actions and "flavor" of the next generation of persons whom we are cultivating as we speak. Immediately gratifying behavior, losing our sense of discipline and treating children as "mini adults" and handing over all control to them, are impending disasters waiting to happen. I believe you all would agree that this has already begun.

If we can begin to understand what "we're about", that we operate from primitive instincts, that we are extremely egocentric and that we come from a basis of individualism, we can begin to understand how other people are thinking and behaving. We also need to understand that there exists a complex interplay between these three variables, and that said interplay can have massive impact on who we are as a society, and what we are producing for the future of this society. This in turn will be the key to having better relations with other people and will help avoid a disaster before its too late.

I believe a select few in this world already understand this process but may not have termed it in the manner that I have. That is, there are some that already have an upper hand in communicating and relating to others.

The secret; one only need to understand that most people are consumed with themselves----and you only need "know something about that," to effectively communicate with them. I conduct this experiment all the time. I will purposefully ask others, "How's it going?"

This open ended opportunity allows another to completely dump their stuff on me because "I asked for it." I also know that most people have something at the ready in their minds that's (a) bothering them----some threat to the self or (b) some accomplishment or conquering that they have achieved that they would like to pontificate to others. Either way, I sit and listen and they will go on and on----I in turn give good eye contact, shake my head in agreement occasionally, and intermittently say "wow," "sure," etc.

By the end of the conversation, they have received affirmation because I have listened and they can now walk away feeling like they really accomplished something good today. I in turn am now viewed as a "nice guy," "a good listener" and an all around good person---and I did nothing but shake my head and utter 2-3 words.

Isn't this amazing? Sales people are very well aware of this phenomena—they may not be able to describe the process in psychological terms, but they do know that people are typically consumed with their own "stuff" and one only need listen to that problem/occurrence, etc, and then offer a solution or product that can solve the issue. "You need an equity line sir----why should you have to be in debt, you're better than that." Bada boom, bada bing—where do I sign up."

Perhaps that is some of the reasons that sales people are not always viewed as the most ethical folks in the world. They manipulate and prey on the very thing that we know least about ourselves------"ourselves." We should not take this lightly however. Why? Well, if this practice of promoting the self becomes sophisticated and more frequent, it becomes more solidified as a way of existence.

Consequently, if our innate need for egocentricism becomes too strong and/or begins to blend with our strong sense of primitivism, we are left with a scary prospect for the future. It's almost a twisting of occurrences if you will. What begins to develop is an alternate mechanism than the one we discussed earlier. If you recall, it is easy to understand how terrorist like activity can occur; a depriving environment forces a coming together for the satisfying of primitive needs (a collective egocentricism if you will).

Again, we saw some of this activity during the 911 era; people in the United States coming together to combat terrorism. If however, the ego becomes too strong, reinforced and unchecked, we begin to see a society that is focused on the self, and begins to engage in primitive like behavior to fulfill and meet this need. Aggression, murder and the like are on the rise in this country. Not because there is war or deprivation, but because there is a significant "clashing of ego's." The self is inflated to the point where many believe themselves to be invincible, and anyone or anything that gets in the way, must be treated accordingly. The real scary part is that we are training this method to our children.

Most developmental psychologists and physicians know that the first 10 years of life are critical on many levels; nutrionally, physically (maturation) and emotionally/behaviorally. If one is exposed to an environment that teaches them to expect everything NOW, and to honor thyself before anyone or anything else, one develops into a large self-loathing, egocentric adult who is consumed with himself and the obtaining of self gratification.

Media, technology and the gaming community all regularly contribute to this process and help it along that much quicker. Video games and the media teach the child to seek immediate gratification, and amply supplies gratification instantly. This is good and bad; bad because it teaches children to expect everything now and good because it provides children with the "hardwiring" to compete in the future.

I had this argument with a school teacher once. She was stating that she has noticed that there are an increasing number of students who are diagnosed with ADHD. The recent statistic I saw was as high as 35-40%. She also stated that she thought that parents were losing control over there children, and didn't know how to be parents. She was not prepared for me.

I began by stating the following; the reason for the steady increase in ADHD is twofold; (1) increased focus on the self and individual pursuits has forced a 2 parent working environment and (2) the result has been "maturation by television". She looked at me with a dumbfounded look because she knew she was in for a lengthy lecture. So, I began......I first explained my theory of individualism leading to egocentrism here in then United States, then explained that when a child is raised by media and video games, the result has developmental effects.

I further explained that when I was a kid, I watched cartoons like Bugs Bunny, Road Runner, etc., and I played video games like Pac Man, Atari, etc. The cartoons and games I frequented were all very slow, deliberate and easy to track. Examine the video games and cartoons of today. Most are fast, very difficult to follow and need a high level of tracking ability to play. My son for example, can track and follow these games without blinking an eye---I just get a headache.

My point to the school teacher? Well, when you put a child who has been raised by television and who has been cognitively trained on Game Boy and the like, you cannot place him back in the middle of Mrs. Johnson's classroom and expect him to follow her writing her lesson plan on the chalkboard. This presentation does not match his maturation and development.

Teachers would be wise to figure out a method to provide additional sources of stimulation in addition to their lesson plans, etc., in order to keep the child's attention. Consequently, if a child is not stimulated enough (Mrs. Johnson's history lesson no longer cuts it), he is going to find ways to stimulate himself-----guess what? He can't help it---he's been hardwired this way, and we have done it to him. So what does he do instead? He pokes, prods, annoys others, talks and gets up from his seat. The diagnosis? ADHD.

Again, this should scare you. Be afraid, be very afraid. I caution everyone reading this book to explore these phenomena and begin to devise ways to influence how we think in this country; particularly when it comes to our children.

What about politics? Has this affected the way we relate to others in the world? What are the basic actions and thought processes' that got us to where we are in today's political arena. I would argue that the basic premise of egocentricism, developed from a strong sense of entitlement and individualism, has gotten us smack dab in the middle of our current conflicts.

How dare anyone come to then United States and attack us---do they know who we are? Obviously, they do not realize who they are dealing with. After all, we are great aren't we? So great in fact that we must help others in the world realize where they are going wrong, and how they can become more like us. We need to intervene to teach others how to become more "democratic" and how to inflate their images of themselves to become healthier human beings.

You see I don't disagree with being a proud nation; that is a very important concept that I would like to see more of. But I do disagree with our casual and convenient use of the words like "nation" and "unity." It seems that the only time we use such words is when we are in the middle of a significant strife or crisis. President Bush will exclaim, "we as a nation are at a turning point---our great NATION was attacked today…….."

My second point is that I do not believe that this process is intentional. As I have mentioned earlier, I think this process occurs subconsciously, and is a very human, primitive behavior that we can only control once we become aware of its presence. We find ourselves seeking gratification, more, more and more, and don't always know why we are doing this? Isn't that wild? It's only when a significant event occurs and jolts us back together again, do we then start talking about how we need to "come together," "work together as one" and "unite as one." Once the strife is gone, it's back to work on ourselves.

We see this happening now; everyone is hopping off the war wagon as quickly as they can; it is again becoming about the self, and our selfish needs. Don't get me wrong, an important view of oneself is an important strength that we all need to posses to compete confidently in today's world. In fact, if we examine the very nature of therapy for one who is depressed or anxious, etc., a therapist will often recommend exercises that are designed to improve the self concept.

For example, a popular reference from Saturday Night Live exemplifies this point; a character played in one of the skits often exclaims as a means of self-re-assurance, "I am good enough, smart enough and gosh darn it, people like me." This is not necessarily a bad thing. If one were to practice this skill long enough, these conscious, practicing thoughts will eventually become subconscious and may run on automation. We should take example from our marketing friends and use their subliminal marketing skills for the betterment of the self rather than for manipulation and greed.

People need to feel comfortable and confident about themselves, otherwise one may find themselves in a state of depression. But how much is too much---when does one become too confident, arrogant and self-absorbed to the point where others around them begin to take note and criticize them as such?

Unfortunately, as we have discussed there is no formal guide or barometer to measure such an escalation or change----if there were, we would see a steady increased reading in this country. Perhaps we need to create a check system; a method for the examination of the self, both individually and collectively in this country.

SO…..WHAT CAN WE DO ABOUT IT?

If all of the above is true, what are the potential effects when all three variables (individualism, egocentricism and primitivism) combine and interact with one another? We already see evidence of such in today's society. We see evidence of technology, media and consumerism changing and altering to accommodate our inflated and growing self of the self. All major fast food restaurants now offer "super sized" options to satisfy our need for more, more and more.

Restaurants as a collective whole have also figured out methods to supply us with this abundance without delay and in an immediate fashion. Why? Because they know, that we know, that we deserve this level of abundance without delay. And, because we feel that we deserve and are owed this level of service and abundance, we also feel entitled to an explanation of why we now are overweight, pre-diabetic and have to pay for rising medical costs to address our over-eating behavior.

In fact, we file lawsuits and blame said fast food restaurants for "making us this way." "It is their fault that I am like this." I was watching a popular morning news program the other day, and they were conducting an interview with a man who is blaming his diabetes on fast food restaurants and the preservatives that they put in their foods. And, he is considering a lawsuit against fast food chains because clearly, it is not his fault. Right?

Where does this level of entitlement come from? What makes us believe that we can demand more, more and more and then bite the very hand that provided the "more?" Evidently, some within the legal field believe these claims to be legitimate and worthy, as a number of folks have filed successful lawsuits acquitting themselves from any responsibility for their OWN behavior. This really cracks me up. For example, if you recall, a person recently filed a lawsuit because he/she was burned from a cup of coffee that was purchased at a local coffee establishment. The jury agreed; this person should have been warned that the small, hot coffee they purchased (and probably has purchased 1000 times before) was HOT.

Further current day evidence includes the increasing use of threats and violence in the school systems as a means of calling attention to oneself. Again, watching a popular morning show, I witnessed two stories talking about young children making bomb threats and/or threatening to endanger others through violent means.

The first child was a "fourth grader," yes, fourth grader, who had written a bomb threat on the bathroom stall. Now where do you suppose he learned that behavior from? Is this something that came to him in a dream or was a well thought out plan, or was this a manifestation of entitlement and an elevated belief of the importance of the self? This was an ingrained belief taught to this child by the society in which he is being raised. Television teaches him to expect everything now, and shows him that such threats or actions are highly publicized and reinforced by adults. Yes adults, the very thing that we all wanted to be when we were kids.

This is not rocket science either; a child wants to be like an adult, so he engages in activities (negative or positive) that he knows adults will attend to. Badda boom, badda bing (no pun intended). The problem; we cover these events and popularize these methods of attention seeking---- nauseatingly so. This repeated coverage----and I mean repeated coverage, makes this child and his cause (as immature and silly as it is), the most important thing in the world for weeks to come. National and international coverage will ensue, and this kid and his cause for righteousness (in his world) is satisfied. "He showed us---- didn't he?" When are we going to wake up and realize this relationship? Because the child believes this to be the most significant issue in the world---and clearly it is in his egocentric world, he has been taught to resort to any means necessary to carry out his mission.

The result often involves primitive like behavior (aggression, violence) to carry out his agenda. Again the scary part is that this is happening more and more, and at younger and younger ages-----we have no one to blame however, but ourselves. We have created our future, but don't quite understand what we have created.

Further complications include the age at which we grant this level of entitlement to our children. As we discussed, children are led to believe that they are privileged to enjoy adult power and entitlement immediately. And we as conforming adults hand over this power and control accordingly. We need to realize that children are not born with the knowledge and skills to help them to mature to healthy and responsible adults. These types of skills are taught to children by guess who----us, as adults. I once talked with a woman who informed me that that she was in the process of teaching her child (8 years old) how to be responsible. Her methodology was as follows; she may pick her bedtime and if she chooses to stay up late, she will be fatigued in the morning, have trouble in school and will consequently learn the skill of responsibility---by consequence if you will.

I honestly had to leave the room because I was about to lose my mind. When I returned, I began my dissertation as follows; Mrs. _____ please bear with me as I explain the process of skill building---as I understand the process to be. A child of 8 years is not born with the innate knowledge to understand the concept of responsibility. A child of 8 years will "learn" responsibility by first having set expectations and structured systems in place that he/she must follow. Once said child has followed set rules and expectations for a long period of time, a funny thing occurs; internalization of this process. Once internalization occurs the child develops a SKILL.

We hand over too much power to children and then expect that they will be able to handle such responsibility. I love the nightly opportunity to tell my daughter and son that it is time for bed. They often respond by stating that they would like to stay up longer and that it is "not fair" that they have to retire now. I will usually rebut back by stating "you need to go to bed now," to which they respond "why," to which I respond by stating "BECAUSE I SAID SO." Got this little trick from my Mom---no explanation needed. I could offer a dissertation to my children which may go something like this---"you see, if you don't get enough sleep you are going to be tired in the morning. Then, when you go to school you will probably have behavior problems because of your fatigue, but you won't necessarily get the connection between your fatigue and your behavior............" I usually don't make it this far into the dissertation because my children will often surrender and ask for a cease fire.

Because we grant such luxuries and entitlement to our children at such early ages, it should come as no surprise that we cannot discipline our children according to "children rules" any longer. As such, we now find ourselves in situations where others are "watching" how we interact with our children and are quick to notify the authorities if they believe we have done something inappropriate. How many times have you seen a parent attempting to discipline their child in the middle of a grocery store? The child is flipping out, throwing themselves on their back and Mom/Dad are forced to show their hands. What do you do? Do you physically discipline? Do you ignore the behavior? Either way, you will be judged and you will be judged severely.

If a parent decides to not "spare the rod" out of fear of spoiling the child, he may be in for a rude awakening. It would not be uncommon for someone viewing this physical intervention to call the police to report abuse. Sadly, I overheard a child communicating with her father once in a store----she was acting inappropriately (demanding, tantruming, etc.) to which he responded by stating, "If you do not stop that, I will spank you right here in front of everyone." Her response----"go ahead, I'll call the police." Clearly in today's world you are dammed if you do and dammed if you don't.

....

Granted, it's great to sit around and pontificate about the idiosyncrasies of the world, but what can we really do about it? Following are some initial suggestions that I think we should begin to consider when addressing such problems. Said suggestions are not the be all and end all of what should occur, but are intended as a "spring board" into necessary discussions about policy and social change that needs to occur before we as a great nation become victims of our own creations.

Firstly.....Obviously, the most dramatic change will come from the sources with the most influence, power and control. The major sources that come to mind are politics, wealth and the majority voice. Dramatic policy and administrative change need to occur on two levels; the first involving foreign policy and the second involving internal, US policy.

Foreign policy needs to alter with the understanding of the basic principles discussed regarding the self, primitivism and the environment; how they all interact and influence each other depending on the condition one finds themselves as it relates to each other. For example, when attempting policy relations with a nation in a state of deprivation, one must assume certain existing conditions. Such assumed conditions would include an immaturely developed id (or sense of the self), a propensity toward a group dynamic, attraction to groups, religions, and/or cults which offer unconditionality and purpose and a strong avocation to complete the identified goals of the group. Sound familiar?

Foreign policy representatives trained and educated within such a format would fair well with international deliberations. Our current system of arrogance and "we are the begin all and end all of knowing," is not working. This change in policy should not be partisan, but should be human. Partisanship as defined in this model is another manifestation of "Americanized egocentricism," and should be viewed as such. It will take much for others to abandon their partisan avocations because it has served them well, on their road to egocentric strength, commodore self-righteousness and wealth.

Regarding internal policy much should begin to domino once the above has begun and is accepted. Internal policy makers in turn should begin to present legislation designed to re-format the family model from its current dysfunctional state, and return it to a model we left behind long ago.

That is, 2 parent homes, family focused designed programs, relief for struggling families so the above can enact, and a general community focus on the family as a group. Albeit, we shouldn't discourage the individual and individual achievement, but clearly there needs to exist a balance of the two. We've seen the results of the individual focus, and most would argue that they are not happy with this model.

Further "trickling" will occur and individual communities will become vested and involved. Individual programs encouraging family involvement should be heavily promoted; children will be pried off their couches and their Game Boys surgically removed from their palms, with only minor sutures needed. Parents and children will communicate once again and television/computers and videogames will serendipitously malfunction and may become irreparable. We will see ourselves as "communities" versus individuals living within a community.

*Secondly........*The wealthy folks in this country really need to get a handle on themselves. How much is enough? How large does the self need to be before one can say, "I made it," "I'm here," "I've arrived." Realizing this need to "feed the id" is insatiable, and that the need for happiness and the avoidance thereof, is also insatiable---are important concepts that need to be implanted in the schema of the wealthy.

One only need ask a very wealthy person how happy they really are?----it must be quite fatiguing engaging in this constant battle of seeking and accruing admiration and wealth, all for the promotion of the self. I would imagine that the stakes become higher, the accreditation harder to obtain and the maintenance of such difficult to sustain, once one reaches such a level of the self.

Here's an outlandish thought; rather than increasing one's net worth to 6 billion versus 5 billion, how about devoting and investing ones knowledge, power, influence and wealth toward a reconstruction of the family unit. Donate to individual community programs that bring families together, support policy makers that support such contentions and make real and fundamental change for our future.

Thirdly......Once absorption and acceptance of these principles has occurred, companies, general work places and leadership should begin to offer incentives for family leave, vacations and time with their families. This is wellness---our previous definitions of wellness in the workplace have focused on the individual---we must shift our perspective to include the family and the group, because when a family is well the individual is well. Somehow, we have reversed the process, and are currently experiencing the negative ramifications of that shift.

Somewhere along the way we as a culture altered our definition of health and wellness and began focusing and convincing others to concern themselves with themselves. Practices such as massage, meditation, spending quality time alone, etc. all sound good on the surface, but what ultimate practice does it promote and teach? I argue that this concentration on the self teaches us to become more focused on our individual needs, and consequently, more demanding for more of this time. We then promote this lifestyle via commercialism and then hammer it into the heads of our children via TV, advertisement, etc. If we teach a child that in order to be "well" you need to take CARE OF YOURSELF, he/she will grow and mature practicing this methodology.

Fourthly.......When are we going to realize the negative effect of sensationalism on inappropriate and violent behavior? When are we going to understand that when we race and compete to cover a violent act like a school shooting, a martyred suicide bomber, etc., we are feeding this need for the promotion of the self. Adapting this model, when one knows he/she can attract massive amounts of attention to the self for completing such an act, we may as well consider it done. People fail to consider that there exists an innate need for attention; when one cannot obtain, and/or is void of positive based attention, he/she will seek it negatively.

I always tell my students…..attention is attention, no matter what the form. I often present the example of my children when I arrive home from work. I walk in the door, and both my children (8 and 11) say, "Dad, come play with us." I respond, "Give me a few minutes; I need to put my bags away, etc......." Twenty minutes passes and I have not returned as I had promised. Suddenly, my wife and I hear a scream and/or "slap" come from the other room. As appropriately responding parents, we both run into the other room to inquire (1) who struck who, (2) who caused such an action to occur and (3) to dole out appropriate consequences. Have they received our attention? -----yes; quite effectively I may add. Is it positively based? No, it was acquired negatively and inappropriately.

Earlier I discussed how such phenomena as egocentricism and primitivism exist often in the subconscious, and subsequent actions are often completed without much forethought. I believe the acquiring of such negative attention exists on a similar plane; my children didn't conference with one another and plan the theatrical act of aggression toward one another knowing the outcome would be immediate parental presence.

Such is the case with the immediate negative attention and promotion of the self that occurs when one commits a horrendous action like a mass shooting. We reinforce such actions and "set the stage" for the next. One only need review such actions and the time line of their occurrences------an expediential increase since Columbine to now. Again, consider the process; one (a neglected, angry child) finds himself in a deprived state (a deprived id), combined with the rejection of the group (no peers=social isolation) results in necessary actions/behaviors for survival (primitivism).

The result; irrational behavior (mass murder, etc.). News/media organizations need to realize their effects on the continuation of this cycle, and change their coverage protocols to discourage rather than reinforce this process----
-someone please stand up! If I had 6 billion dollars, I could change this process-----I would begin by offering, (perhaps doubling) a significant amount of money to the paparazzi group as a whole to photograph acts of kindness, human spirit news and like versus photos of Paris Hilton being carted off to jail.

Further, the very nature of television needs to change. Although I am not that old, I do remember that comedy in the mid 1900's was based on 2 general themes; (1) slapstick humor (Three Stooges and the like) and (2) making fun of the self. Today's comedy is defined on how articulate and effective one can be at insulting and making fun of another. This should be a scary and awakening notation for all of us---for this is how we are teaching our children to interact with others. We wonder why we can't relate to our children. We live in a very sarcastic, intolerant and judgmental society and we have made it as such.

We need to understand and reacquaint ourselves with the founded correlation between observation and action. That is, Bandura (a wise old psychological researcher) demonstrated for us many years ago the strong relationship between the observation of negative behavior and the subsequent repeating of such negative behavior---- rocket science huh? Yep, when children witness, view or observe acts of violence they will repeat. So, here's a bright idea, let's create more sophisticated, realistic, virtual games and television shows that depict violent acts like aggression, bludgeoning, decapitation and murder, and let's make it competitive and available for all.

And, if that weren't enough, let's allow the various advocacy groups defending the "freedom of speech" amendment to tell us as citizens that this freedom of "artistic expression" is more important than the development of our children. Let us all then go off and pursue our own egocentric goals and purposes, and allow such programming to be the sole company for our children. Parents need to unite and put an end to such botchery before it's too late. It's time to wake up America and smell the roses before our children decapitate them with their machetes.

Fifthly..... We need to praise and reinforce one another more often. This is a major void in our current society. We are quick to point out the negative, and "what is wrong" with a situation, but we are "learned deficient" in noting the positive actions of others. One only need take a drive on any American street to see this practice at work. Lord help you if you make a wrong turn at the wrong time, if you don't move quickly enough when the light turns green. If such occurs, we are instantly, intolerably confronted with aggression, agitation and threats of violence for such innocent, unintentional happenings. You are tried, judged and sentenced in a matter of seconds.

Don't stare too long at another, for fear of your life. It sometimes seems like we are playing a game of "stare down chicken" with others. You really want to stare the other person down and show confidence, but are you really prepared for what can occur if the other person decides to do the same? Does it have to be a contest? The fact that we have to debate this philosophical issue should scare all of us.

Often I include as a boiler plate requirement in my programs and recommendations for behaviorally challenged folks, a mandatory reinforcement schedule that must be completed by staff. That is, every half an hour for example, they <u>MUST</u> compliment the person supported in a genuine, positive manner---with genuine being the operative word.

I have found that when one is "flooded" with such kindness and complimentary remarks, one alters their reinforcement needs, and begins to seek such positive affirmation and abandons their previous inappropriate need for negative attention. It is quite remarkable how effective this process can be. This makes me believe that movies like "Pay It Forward" are a necessary ingredient to fix our tattered society.

We must understand that all human beings have the potential to be "good." That is, we all seek the same basic things in life. Our previous discussion regarding affirmation and happiness are good examples of this common need. Affirmation and attention equal feelings of happiness, and most would agree that once one is able to move beyond our "tough exteriors," remove us from our "battle tanks" (aka our cars) and communicate, we often change our first impressions of others. We say things like, "he's not so bad after all," "once you get to know her, she's a nice person isn't she?" We need to slow down and take the time to communicate again. I am convinced that the reason we are seeing increases in psychiatric diagnoses, increased inter-relational problems and increased conflict in the world is because of our progressing "turning inward" toward a focus on the individual and a straying from others.

Those who are incapable of handling this "turn inward" are often left to work out their issues on their own. This may explain some of the increases in our intolerance of folks dependent of welfare, the homeless population and others in need of general assistance and services. In today's world we are not very understanding of these people and will often ignore, ostracize and criticize their dependence on such services and charity. It is remarkable to me that in today's world-----when the money gets tight, the first cuts and decreases often occur to the populations who cannot advocate for themselves. Persons with disabilities, the homeless and welfare recipients often come to mind.

When we remove the opportunity from another to belong and feel included with others, we remove affirmation and attention and we produce unhappiness. Because we are all survivors and primitive beings, we have the ability to self preserve. Self-preservation can take many forms and is often guided by our need to feel good again. If

I as a human being cannot get this need from others, I will follow suit and turn inward in my thoughts and actions. Again we see example of this practice in general society. People will self-medicate; alcohol, anti-depressants, and food.

I often become angry when working with other service providers who seek to completely "clinicize" and control a person with a disability. Usually the criticism surrounds a persons eating habits; the person seeks food and does not have control over their intake. I ask "what sources of happiness does this person have?" They live in a 24 hour environment with staff, have limited connection to the community and are often judged because of their disability. In such cases, I believe that people will self preserve and seek methods of happiness that are available and accessible. Food proves to be an effective self medication tool in this example.

We need not limit ourselves to review of the disability community to see this practice in action. Obesity statistics in the United States has exploded in the last 10-20 years. Why? As we are forced and pushed toward a continued focus on ourselves, we have to accept all that may "come with the package." There will be those that can handle this focus on the self and will thrive, and there will be others who cannot control and/or discipline their behavior and will have issues. Obesity has skyrocketed because there are those that cannot regulate their eating behaviors and have completely bought into the "righteous belief" that they deserve every last French fry on that "super sized" platter.

We need to stop viewing the indigent in this Country as slackers, useless human beings and leaches of society. Granted there are abuses of the system, but continued ostracizing and segregation of others for their faults only causes increased desperate attempts at self-preservation, and creates a general negative opinion of anyone who resembles this profile. The result---look around. Homeless families on the street, people lying in the middle of the road, open violence, etc.

Good Morning America recently presented a story and video clip where an elderly man was struck by a car in Connecticut and lay in the road for minutes before a police officer happened upon the incident. The video also showed numerous people walking and driving by the man, and nobody approached to help. What is wrong with U.S.?

Lastly.....We need to come to some collective agreement regarding technology, the use and proliferation of technology and the potential effects on our children. Additionally, we need to come to some agreement of how this technology should change and modify current teaching methodologies and curriculums in our school systems. If we don't, I fear that we will continue with our current process of diagnostics (ADHD, Oppositional Defiance Disorder, Conduct Disorder, etc.) and will continue with our trend toward medicating children to solve the immediate problem, versus investing our time and resources to solve the real fundamental issue.

As I discussed earlier, I believe that our current curricular system has not caught up with the excelled version of cognitive hardwiring that our children are developing. Because of this level of sophistication and hard wiring, our children are having difficulty attending to "Mrs. Johnson" when she is presenting her dissertation on the revolutionary war. It's not that the child doesn't "get" what the teacher is saying; the child is not stimulated enough "to attend." There is a major difference between the two. I may be intelligent enough to understand what a teacher is attempting to teach, but I do not comprehend what she is saying because the presentation is not stimulating enough to keep my attention. Remember, our children of today are watching television shows and playing video games that are fast moving, incredibly stimulating and difficult to track and follow. I challenge any baby boomer to watch an episode on Nickelodeon or the like, and I guarantee you will struggle to attend to the content. We should begin to understand that the reverse also holds true, when we present a current day child with "our" understanding of what content is appropriate for them, they cannot attend either.

We need to re-design classrooms to "catch up" to the new millennium. Researchers need to begin exploration as to how exactly that may look. For example, I often wondered how a class of diagnosed ADHD kids would fair in a classroom where there existed multiple levels of "manufactured stimulation" in addition to "Mrs. Johnson's" dissertation? Examples could include flat screens in the front of the room displaying background "miscellaneous activity" where the child would now perhaps focus as a result. If this theory were correct, the child would not be distracted, but stimulated enough to now attend to what she was saying. The activity could not be meaningful activity, as it may prove a distraction. I believe a great deal of time should be invested in this exploration as stories are numerous of needless medicating and "snowing" children to quiet their minds.

We also have to accept that the revolution against ridding the world of this level of technology is not going to work. Technology will continue to progress with or without us, and our children will be using this technology to create countless new discoveries. In twenty years I believe all computer related technology will be virtual. Our children will need to have this base level of hardwiring to compete in such an environment. We cannot therefore, abandon any training that such technology is providing for this inevitable occurrence. We can however control its use and shape access to this knowledge in appropriate and functional ways. In order to fix our current situation we have to abandon this righteous fight against this level of technology----it's too late. Synaptic pathways have been created and many children now *need* this level of stimulation to attend normally.

I am not advocating for 24 hour Game Boy sessions on the couch, but I do think we need to create some moderate access to such technology. As I mentioned earlier, we need to pry our children from their television sets and video games in order to begin thinking about restoring our society back to a tolerant, kind and humane existence. Perhaps we should think about the school day and how we can modify this time to give access to technology. This would allow us more controls over content and allow us an opportunity to make such sessions productive. Increased family involvement should also aid with the "prying" that needs to occur.

In conclusion, I would say to all of you, "IMAGINE WHAT A WORLD THIS COULD BE," not "WHAT CRAZY WORLD THIS IS." I think it's time to wake up America---let's recognize ourselves and make fundamental changes before it's too late.

What's wrong with U.S.?